Reflections
on
Canadian Character

Reflections
on
Canadian Character

From Monarch Park to
Monarch Mountain

Bob Couchman

BREAKOUT EDUCATIONAL NETWORK
IN ASSOCIATION WITH
DUNDURN PRESS
TORONTO · OXFORD

Publisher: Inta D. Erwin
Copy-editor: Maggie MacDonald, First Folio Resource Group
Production Editor: Amanda Stewart, First Folio Resource Group
Designer: Bruna Brunelli, Brunelli Designs
Printer: Webcom

National Library of Canada Cataloguing in Publication Data

Couchman, Robert
  Reflections on Canadian character: from Monarch Park to
Monarch Mountain/by Bob Couchman.

One of the 16 vols. and 14 hours of video which make up the
  underground royal commission report.
Includes bibliographical references and index.
ISBN 1-55002-430-2

  1. Canada — Social policy. 2. Public welfare — Canada. 3. National
characteristics, Canadian. I. Title. II. Title: underground royal
commission report.

HV108.C674 2002   361.6'1'0971   C2002-902310-6

1   2   3   4   5   07   06   05   04   03

Printed and bound in Canada.
Printed on recycled paper. ♻
www.dundurn.com

Exclusive Canadian broadcast rights for the *underground royal commission* report

intelligent television

Check your cable or satellite listings for telecast times

Visit the *urc* Web site link at:
www.ichanneltv.com

The *underground royal commission* Report

Since September 11, 2001, there has been an uneasy dialogue among Canadians as we ponder our position in the world, especially vis à vis the United States. Critically and painfully, we are re-examining ourselves and our government. We are even questioning our nation's ability to retain its sovereignty.

The questions we are asking ourselves are not new. Over the last 30 years, and especially in the dreadful period of the early 1990s, leading up to the Quebec referendum of 1995, inquiries and Royal commissions, one after another, studied the state of the country. What *is* new is that eight years ago, a group of citizens looked at this parade of inquiries and commissions and said, "These don't deal with the real issues." They wondered how it was possible for a nation that was so promising and prosperous in the early 60s to end up so confused, divided, and troubled. And they decided that what was needed was a different kind of investigation — driven from the grassroots 'bottom,' and not from the top. Almost as a provocation, this group of people, most of whom were affiliated with the award winning documentary-maker, Stornoway Productions, decided to do it themselves — and so was born the *underground royal commission*!

What began as a television documentary soon evolved into much more. Seven young, novice researchers, hired right out of university, along with a television crew and producer, conducted interviews with people in government, business, the military and in all walks of life, across the country. What they discovered went beyond anything they had expected. The more they learned, the larger the implications grew. The project continued to evolve and has expanded to include a total of 23 researchers over the last several years. The results are the 14 hours of video and 16 books that make up the first interim report of the *underground royal commission*.

So what *are* the issues? The report of the *underground royal commission* clearly shows us that regardless of region, level of government, or political party, we are operating under a wasteful system ubiquitously lacking in accountability. An ever-weakening connection between the electors and the elected means that we are slowly and irrevocably losing our right to know our government. The researchers' experiences demonstrate that it is almost impossible for a member of the public, or in most cases, even for a member of Parliament, to actually trace how our tax dollars are spent. Most disturbing is the fact that our young people have been stuck with a crippling IOU that has effectively hamstrung their future. No wonder, then, that Canada is not poised for reaching its potential in the 21st century.

The *underground royal commission* report, prepared in large part by and for the youth of Canada, provides the hard evidence of the problems you and I may long have suspected. Some of that evidence makes it clear that, as ordinary Canadians, we are every bit as culpable as our politicians — for our failure to demand accountability, for our easy acceptance of government subsidies and services established without proper funding in place, and for the disservice we have done to our young people through the debt we have so blithely passed on to them. But the real purpose of the *underground royal commission* is to ensure that we better understand how government processes work and what role we play in them. Public policy issues must be understandable and accessible to the public if they are ever to be truly addressed and resolved. The *underground royal commission* intends to continue pointing the way for bringing about constructive change in Canada.

— Stornoway Productions

14 hours of videos also available with the *underground royal commission* report.
Visit Stornoway Productions at www.stornoway.com for a list of titles.

Table of Contents

"For my children, Barbara, Stephen and Michael, who share my passion for social justice, and my grandchildren, Frances, Matthew, Ruth and Sam, who will hopefully benefit from our efforts."

Foreword

The social landscape of Canada is as much a part of our society's natural evolution as our economic and political course. Bob Couchman, who grew up poor in Toronto's east end during the late Depression years and World War II, tells his story of change from a social perspective. Bob is great with kids and his natural talents led him to work as a camp counsellor and school teacher; he was also one of Toronto's original detached youth workers assigned to work with delinquent gangs in the back alleys of east Toronto. His perspective on the creation and decline of Canada's version of the welfare state is pragmatic — a view from the trenches, rather than academia. Even when he rose to become CEO of Canada's largest family service agency, a foundation president and Canadian co-chair for the UN's International Year of the Family, his prime concern remained with individuals and families. Most recently this concern has taken Couchman to the Yukon, where he continues to work directly on behalf of both Aboriginal and non-Aboriginal people. Because of his frontline perspective, he has also become an advisor to the federal government and provincial and territorial governments.

Couchman is in a unique position to offer a before-and-after picture of the two worlds in which he has lived. The inception of the Canadian welfare state in the late 1940s and early 1950s was both a reflection and an integral part of the development of our national character. Recently Canadian character has again changed dramatically, thus leading to the dismantling of social programs. Couchman speaks from a vantage point congruent with the explorations of the *underground royal commission.*

As governments and professionals became the principal deliverers of social services and programs, there was a waning of the sense of personal reciprocal obligation that his parents and grandparents felt so strongly. Couchman notes that the early programs of the welfare state were rooted in a balance between public and government responsibility. At the time no one talked of rights. They talked of individual and collective responsibility and obligation to one another. His is no simplistic indictment of the welfare state, the kind of slash-and-burn approach one might get from a person concerned only with fiscal responsibility. He praises the introduction of collective social programs as they significantly reduced the hit-and-miss tendencies of informal personal systems of care. On the other hand, as these collective systems of care became the norm, they became deeply entrenched in political, public and professional self-interest. Political bureaucracy and professional elites gradually fossilized the systems of care, making it impossible for continued natural evolution. Couchman notes with considerable poignancy that little heed is given to the real effectiveness of social programs. Do they in fact meet the real needs of individuals and families?

Underlying Couchman's life story is real rebellion against the phenomenon of resistance to change. As he notes, resistance to change became an inherent part of the welfare state — and contributed the death blow to the vision and dreams of the public and political leaders who worked so hard to bring equity and justice to the Canadian social landscape. His final message, however, is far from one of hopelessness. He witnesses new social developments and public attitudes that offer promise for the future social landscape of Canada. "We have always been a people who looked after one another when times were tough. While the systems and institutions we've developed during the past 50 years may not be up to the challenge of reform, there are forces already at work which will sweep aside intransigent obsolescence and create a new social order."

Patrick Boyer

Chapter 1

A Cardboard Sole

She'd now become quite adept with the task, cutting out cardboard soles, perfect size fives. The woman then inserted the soles into the child's shoes. "There," she said to herself, "that should cover the holes and keep a little warmth wrapped around the child's feet." The year was 1918, the location Reid Street in downtown Toronto. The mother was my grandmother and the child my mother. As always for the family, these were difficult times, though an improvement over life in the one-room sod hut on the Saskatchewan prairies. My mother was a week old when she came from the hospital in Moose Jaw to live in the hut with her two brothers, my grandfather and my grandmother. My grandfather, among many other things, was a failed homesteader.

This particular episode ended abruptly when my mother was six months of age. My aunt Ethel came to visit her sister and immediately decided to load the three children and my grandmother aboard a day coach on the Trans Canada Railway. No Bigelow was to live in that squalor. They returned to Toronto leaving my grandfather another few months struggling to till the land. Finally the ox drowned in a slough and he gave up in discouragement.

The child grew impatient wanting to go outdoors and play with the other girls. The mend now completed, she put on her shoes and raced out into the street to skip. There was another little girl out there who, believe it or not, was even worse off. Her feet were bound in rags, as she had no shoes. Following my grandmother's gentle nature, my mother had been profoundly moved by her friend's plight.

With winter coming, the day came to purchase new shoes. They were certainly nothing elegant. "Serviceable," my grandfather described them. My mother went outside to show them to her friends. She returned at day's end, barefoot. She had given her new shoes to her friend. When my grandfather went into a rage, grandmother, as she would inevitably do throughout their marriage, calmed him. My grand-mother understood my mother's generosity, as she suffered from the same inclination: if someone is worse off than you, you try to help them. That winter many more cardboard soles had to be cut for those old shoes.

This story found its way into my mental archives along with the one about my uncle, as a boy, pulling his wagon to the nearby gas works to sort through the used coke. Among the cinders he'd find some precious pieces not yet burned. When the wagon was fully loaded, he'd haul it home to supply the stove, the family's one source of heat. As with all the houses on Reid Street there were no indoor toilets. You would go to the bottom of the garden to the outhouse. There you would find the Eaton's catalogue and rip off another page or two. Possibly the most momentous day in the family's life occurred when they moved to their new home with indoor toilet facilities and a tub with running cold water. I'm not sure how they heated the water for bathing, but it was probably done as it was during my childhood years. You'd heat up the large kettle on the stove until it was boiling and then pour the contents into a washbasin half filled with cold water. If you wanted a bath, then you lit the Rudd Heater in the basement. After an hour the water in the tank would be hot toward the top and warm at the bottom. I recall my father testing the tank by touching the top to see whether the water had reached the right temperature. If so, the gas would be turned off immediately to save precious pennies. Then the bath would be poured.

Most Canadian families can recall similar stories told by their great-grandparents and grandparents. While many of these tales recount life in Canada in the early to middle part of the 20th century, many other Canadians are regaled with family stories that took place in Europe, Asia, Africa or the Caribbean. They are common stories, however. They tell of triumph overcoming physical and often mental adversity. The experiences contained in these stories are from the roots of Canadian character and culture.

The story I tell is one of the millions of personal histories which make up the Canadian character. Only my age makes my particular story different from most, as I am now a grandparent who lived at that moment in history when the Canadian social programs were first introduced. Thus, I experienced life prior to the advent of employment insurance, medicare, social-support programs, disability support and the host of other social programs that became part of the fabric of Canadian life. Unlike most of my east Toronto contemporaries, who entered the manufacturing and construction trades of booming post-war Canada, I chose a career in helping to deliver the more personal of these social programs. As a result, I witnessed and participated in the rapid expansion of the Canadian welfare state as a soldier in the trenches. Unlike most of the social policy colleagues who participated in the evolution of these programs from the security of government ministries or academia, my overview of the rise and fall of the Canadian welfare state was conditioned by personal experiences and observations made at the frontline. This is certainly not to say that my account of what transpired is more valid than that of the policy analysts. In fact, it may well be that their knowledge of specific program elements can be more accurately detailed than my own. On the other hand, I was able to observe first hand the gap between the intent and the actual achievement, or lack thereof, of that intent. Much of my story deals with the failure of this intent. My mother would often chide me as a child. It was what I did, rather than any intentions, that ultimately mattered. In this respect, at 89 years of age my mother continues to point out the anomalies. I'm sure she also wonders how it is that her son couldn't get it right, despite having this important principle "drilled into his mind."

While this is very much a Canadian story, it reflects the floundering of good intentions and the mixed outcomes of those intentions. It's a story that can be told of other Western democracies, as well as Australia and New Zealand. Thus, while specific details vary from country to country, the same development and inevitable transition of social programs has occurred in almost all social-welfare states. I cannot, however, speak to the experiences of countries other than my own.

At age 65 I should be wandering "gently into that good night" of my career. However, being a person of perpetual passion, I find it difficult to be content with simple retirement. No doubt deciding to settle in the Yukon Territory in my later years is a manifestation of the determination I have felt to live a full and vigorous life. Unlike most of the social-work colleagues who came to their work professionally trained, I came into the field as a volunteer when I was 16 years of age. Upon entering Queen's University summer school, I chose to pursue philosophy rather than subjects more closely related to my eventual vocation. While this academic choice may seem strange, it felt right at the time. I now have little doubt that this choice provided the motivation to constantly ask fundamental questions about my work. This interest in philosophy gradually provided me with the inclination to ask the larger questions about the directions my career was taking, and whether the unfolding of universal social programs was achieving the goals that the families and legislators of the 1930s, 1940s and 1950s intended.

In the end, however, that image of my grandmother cutting cardboard soles for my mother's shoes, and the unquestioning sacrifice made by my mother in giving up her new shoes to a friend in greater need, became my value heritage and, alas, my burden. It's against the cultural backdrop of the thousands upon thousands of neighbourly deeds and sacrifices that our forefathers and foremothers undertook that Canadian social programs emerged. Our grandparents and great-grandparents had no romantic illusions as to the benefits of their generosity. Times were tough in the 1930s. As a result, you simply did what you could to alleviate the suffering of those in even greater need than yourself. It was your inherent duty.

Despite these best efforts, however, far too many people fell through the gaps. Social programs were therefore put into place to take up the slack under exceptional circumstances. The concept of universality existed only insofar as any individual or family experiencing severe hardship should be hungry or be without shelter. No sense of entitlement existed in those early years. The character of Canadians was proud, and few people wanted to suffer the disgrace of having to go on welfare. As we will see, when Canadian character changed, personal responsibility and the sense of social obligation as tangible Canadian values were eclipsed. This is not to say they disappeared. At some level they continue to exist, emerging from the shadows when some major tragedy or compelling personal need occurs. A major flood, a fire, an ice storm and the stranding of thousands of travellers in Newfoundland on September 11, 2001, elicited a compassionate and generous response from Canadians. Nevertheless, Canadians seem less conscious of the daily suffering that surrounds them. We pass homeless people on the streets and pass bylaws to eliminate squeegee kids from the streets. My mother recalls, as the elders in many Canadian families will recall, the occasional hobo being invited into the kitchen for soup and a sandwich before continuing on his journey in search of a job. Likewise, there are countless stories of generosity and kindness that continue to be told to grandchildren and great-grandchildren by the elders in their family. Sadly, we often do not listen carefully to these stories, as they tell of times when acts of kindness were taken for granted. Such acts were what good people did for neighbours and for the strangers in their midst. It was a change in these attitudes and values, indeed a change in the Canadian character, that slowly altered the principles underlying our social-welfare programs. This character change shifted us from a moral sense of reciprocal obligation to a firm belief in entitlement. It was this sense of entitlement that provided the fertilizer for the growth of universality. Thus, with fundamental character change, the seeds for the demise of the Canadian welfare state were sown.

Chapter 2

Laneways, Alleys
and
Childhood Dreams

Alan was asleep on the couch when I came home from an assignment in Toronto. Alan was 10 years old, a member of the Tlingit community in the town of Atlin in northwest British Columbia. We lived on the side of Monarch Mountain, just outside the town of Atlin, from 1996 until 1999, following a move from Toronto. After several years living with a foster family in Watson Lake, Alan was returned to his father's custody in Atlin. Alan's dad was a middle-aged father, like myself. As he had never been solely responsible for his son, Alan's care was informally shared by other Tlingit families, the local school and non-Native neighbours, such as my wife, Carolyn, and me. He thrived comfortably in our close-knit community of family, friends and neighbours after his tumultuous early childhood. Watching him play with our son Michael and other children, there seemed little to set him apart from other neighbourhood youngsters.

Oddly enough, it was one of the last years of the 20th century, a point at which Canada's social-service system had evolved into a sophisticated array of regulations, professional standards and therapeutic expertise. And yet here we had a situation in which the old African saying "It takes a community to raise a child" remained the best way to help this child.

As I looked at Alan trustingly sleeping on the couch and, later, eagerly eating at our dinner table between outbursts of boyish giggles and secret references only known to himself and Michael, I recollected a similar setting in east Toronto 50 years ago.

Andrew, a neighbour's son, used to drop by our home when his mother was in a rage. Still sharp in my memory is Andrew's mom chasing him down the alleyway between the houses while beating him about the head and shoulders with a broom. Andrew eventually ended up in St. John's Training School after sexually assaulting a neighbour's daughter. In some twisted turn of the Canadian justice system, there he too became a victim of sexual abuse. My mother's response to the abuse he suffered was simply to feed and protect Andrew, while quietly suggesting to his mother that the boy could use a little more love in place of frequent beatings. At that point in my young life I had never heard of the Children's Aid Society, nor, for her part, had my mother. Even if we had, it would have been difficult for my parents to call it, as we had no phone in our working-class home. Aside from the Broadview YMCA and a local scout troop, we knew nothing about social agencies or professional social workers.

Between these two episodes some 50 years apart, I was to learn a great deal more about Canada's social programs. My life journey was to take me from the back lanes, pool halls and side streets of east Toronto, where I served as a YMCA detached youth worker working with delinquent street gangs, to the floor of the General Assembly of the United Nations. I was credentialed by External Affairs to be part of the Canadian delegation when I served as co-chair of the Canada Committee for the International Year of the Family in 1994. My vocational wanderings were to encompass teaching elementary school, directing Canada's oldest and largest family-service agency, lecturing graduate students in education at the University of Toronto, chairing Outward Bound Canada and directing one of Canada's larger private foundations. Having done it all, so to speak, I now enjoy northern living as a resident of Whitehorse, Yukon, and part-time resident of nearby Atlin, B.C. I still make forays to urban centres in Canada and the U.S., where I continue to work in a consulting capacity with social-service organizations, as well as advise a medium-sized national private foundation.

I was born in 1937. From St. Michael's Hospital I was taken to my parents' flat on Withrow Avenue in Toronto's east end. Six months later my parents moved into their modest five-room house on nearby Rhodes Avenue in the Monarch Park neighbourhood. The house cost them $2,800 and they took a 25-year mortgage to pay it off. Dad worked as a lawn bowl mechanic for a small company in lower Cabbagetown. I recall his unique vocation always drew questions from classmates when I was asked at school about my father's occupation.

While I was too young to have any sense of the Great Depression, I do recall my maternal grandmother, standing in the archway between our postage-stamp-sized living room and equally modest dining room, breaking the news to my mother that a war had started in Europe. The air must have been electric with anxiety. I was only two and a half when this happened. Obviously I had no concept of war, but my grand- mother and mother certainly remembered the "Great War." As one might expect, the emotional climate of our home was chronically anx- ious, a consequence of the frail economic hold that working-class fam- ilies in our neighbourhood had on their security. An illness, accident or suddenly being laid off from work inevitably spelt financial disaster. Fortunately such personal crises were rare.

My childhood was haunted by the shadow of the Great Depression. Chronic admonitions to "eat everything on your plate" and to "save half your paper route money for your education" were reminders of more difficult times. We were, of course, reassured that we would never have to face such poverty again. Mom's mantra in response to this insecurity was, "You know your father would give you the shirt off his back if he ever had to." Gradually I became aware of the significance of this pro- nouncement. My mother would also occasionally tell my brother and me stories of her childhood household, stories where often the little meat on the table went to my grandfather: "Those who work in the fam- ily need to be fed." It seemed she was never far from her birthplace, in that single-room sod hut on the Saskatchewan prairie. The crop failure that forced her family to move back east when she was only six months of age was a lasting reference point for success and failure in life.

Of course, the war years in Canada brought a new level of prosper- ity to our neighbourhood. For the first time in over a decade everyone had a job, including my mother and a number of her women friends. At the same time the radio and the newspapers gave ominous reports on battles lost and major retreats during those first couple of years of the Second World War. People didn't want to discuss the distinct possibility that we might lose the war, as they had lived too long with threats over their heads. Unlike today, when we recognize the spin placed on pronouncements emanating from Ottawa, Canadians in 1939 to 1945 embraced the propaganda without question. There could be no room for public doubt.

The BBC news was carried direct from Great Britain. During silent moments in my grandparents' living room on Sundays, I recall the squawks, occasional overlaying of Morse code and rise and fall of the very British voice, as the green eye of the tuner opened and closed. I was also sensitive to the now familiar anxiety. The future was never far from everyone's consciousness.

After the BBC broadcast there would be discussion among the men of the family about what was happening in Europe. If debate erupted, my grandfather always had the final word over my uncle George and my dad. After all, he had served in the British artillery just prior to the First World War, so I was impressed that he knew about strategies and military matters. In the meantime, my grandmother, aunt and mother would prepare the joint in the kitchen, this meat having been discreetly contributed to the meal by my parents. My father and mother had jobs.

I was told on such family occasions that you didn't discuss money, confidential family matters or religion, as those topics were no one's business, even among close family members. This was such a strong edict that my father didn't even realize that my grandmother wasn't his real mother until he was grown up and had to apply for his birth certificate. It was only then that he discovered his mother had died in childbirth. Being of English stock, such matters were not discussed.

Stiff, blue, circular meat tokens. Ration books. Collecting tinfoil from cigarette packages. Burlap bags with milkweed pods sitting on the school fence to dry, later to be used as filling for life jackets. The purchase of war stamps. Printed instructions on what to do in the event of an air raid, hanging inside the front door. These are my childhood memories of Canada at war.

My toys, as a small child, were limited as much by the lack of materials as by the fact that toys were very much a luxury item for our family.

I had some metal soldiers in khaki uniforms, all of whom were, alas, standing at attention. This made it difficult to enact action-filled battles in the dirt holes, which substituted for foxholes, at the bottom of our neighbourhood gardens. My real treasures as a child were German war souvenirs, sent to me in lumpy, brown, paper-covered packages from my dad's friend "Uncle Harold." Harold drove an ambulance in the Italian campaign. The prizes among my possessions were a leather German cartridge belt, followed by the burned-out element of some sort of incendiary device. I also had a small collection of aluminum serial-number plates from German and Italian vehicles and planes, for which I could find little use. Once, a faded letter containing a flower arrived, written in beautiful German script. I recall my parents being very unsettled by this souvenir, and it was taken from me and placed in the top drawer of their bureau, along with the bankbooks, insurance policy and other important household papers. Until then the Nazis, as we had come to call them, were not real people with families and loved ones. My perception of the human race inched away from the stereotypes that our propaganda would have us believe. Raised on a diet of official prejudice, it is now difficult for a number of my generation to adapt with open minds to multiculturalism.

Jack Davidson, Dennis Thompson, Bob Gautrey and I re-enacted all the important battles of the war from the foxholes dug in the bush perimeter of Monarch Park or leaping from roof to roof on the garages in the laneway behind Rhodes Avenue. I was always decked out with my prized cartridge belt and wooden rifle. In tight spots we would unleash the incendiary device as a grenade to clear our path, and then would spend several minutes searching for its recovery. It certainly found greater action in Monarch Park and in the laneways than it ever had on that battlefield in southern Italy. In fact, Jack Davidson was so influenced by the subject of our play and the war ethos that he became an RCAF fighter pilot in the late 1950s. The war influenced us both directly and indirectly, it seems.

The reality of the war seemed millions of miles away from our little gang and the material sacrifices that our parents were having to make, despite the constant news from the fronts. I recall we put together something called "ditty bags" for sailors. I have a vivid recollection of the ditty bags from kindergarten and Grade 1. They were navy blue and about the size of a large purse. Into these bags we would bring candy bars, our mothers' knitted socks and gloves, always a harmonica and, finally, cigarettes. I developed a sense that our sailors must have quite a concert orchestra of harmonicas. Eventually the bag would be filled to overflowing. Miss Gibson, our kindergarten teacher, would pull the white drawstring and the ditty bag would be sent off to our sailors at sea.

There had, of course, been almost 10 years of sacrifice leading up to the war, so the values of sacrifice, saving and responsibility were ingrained into our characters at a tender age. This was our way of life in east Toronto. Family pleasures were few: a walk on Sundays, the only day my father didn't work, listening to *Amos and Andy*, *Superman*, and *Terry and the Pirates* on radio, and filling our hours with friends and fantasy. I recall a number of years later hiking through the Himalayan foothills on my way to a climb. I came across a village in which the children were playing. A child had made a plane out of two crossed sticks and had fastened a paper propeller to the front of the plane with a pin. When the child ran with the plane the propeller rotated in the breeze. I recall the scene prompted a flashback to my childhood years.

While we didn't realize it, we were children of the working class. We knew our place in the community and the expectation that we would find good jobs as skilled labourers. The wealth and lifestyles of the privileged class living across the Bloor Viaduct, in Rosedale, might as well have been a million miles away.

With my adult understanding, I can now look back to these formative childhood years in the midst of the war crisis and see that great value was given to social solidarity. Our character was moulded by the turmoil and anxiety of a nation at war and imprinted with parental memories of the financial insecurity bred by the Great Depression. As children, however, we were oblivious to the subtle influences of these two occurrences. Nevertheless, these events dominated our parents' lives. Our parents, in turn, passed on their values in a very firm manner to each of us. We thus became the seeds for our parents' lost hopes and dreams. This placed incredible expectations upon each of us. We were also, however, viewed as valued individuals. Many were the times our teachers, the clergy and our parents would remind us that we were Canada's greatest resource. The sacrifice made by our families and Canadian soldiers for our welfare and futures was very tangible.

As to our own small sacrifices, we saw these as real achievements and were proud when, for example, we completed the filling of our war stamps book. The stamps were 25¢ each and it took forever to fill the pages of the book. We were assured, however, that we would get our money back with about one percent interest when we won the war. It made us proud that we were contributing to the national cause, and we were humbled by the constant reminder that our war stamp book was a modest contribution when compared to the real sacrifices being made overseas by our brothers, sisters and dads.

Thus, we lived in a culture where one's duty to family, neighbours and country was the dominant value. While I am sure that rights existed, little was ever said of them. Certainly as a child I was given a few simple privileges, such as my 25¢ weekly allowance and being allowed to ride my secondhand bicycle on the road when I was 10 years of age. These privileges were earned through being responsible and doing one's duty. I never considered them as rights. As far as I can recall the only right that was held out as a reward was that of being able to vote when we became 21 years of age. And even this democratic right was positioned as a fundamental duty of citizenship. Without noticing it, our culture would gradually change over the next couple of decades. Duty and responsibility as fundamental cultural values would herald the age of rights and freedoms.

One day the blinds were pulled in Mrs. Beer's house and the neighbours began the ritual of taking pies and casseroles to her door and staying for a cup of tea. In those days the casseroles were coated with toasted bread crumbs rather than the cashews of the 1950s. Mr. Beer had been "lost in action." I recall his son Jack, who was older than our gang, was very confused by the situation. He hadn't seen his dad in four years and had not, therefore, realized his dad's importance to his family. As most of us had older dads who were on the home front, we identified more with his loss than perhaps he did. It was a frightening prospect. When we sang "O God Our Help in Ages Past" on Remembrance Day, we knew personally that we were living in real time. Mr. McCall, our principal at Earl Haig Public School, then read out the names of our school's dead graduates in a solemn voice. More than a few of us had tears in our eyes. The family names were almost all familiar to us.

One day in the middle of the fall term Clarence entered our class. He had arrived from one of the cities in the English Midlands which had been the target of German bombs. Like many urban British youngsters sent to the countryside or to Canada for their safety, Clarence quickly became the centre of considerable attention as he described the trip across the Atlantic in an empty troop ship dodging enemy U-boats. The best part of Clarence's story was, however, the bomb crater in the school yard that greeted the children upon return to school one morning. Alas, the bomb missed the school by only a few yards.

I had the good fortune to walk with Clarence to and from Sunday school, which we attended at the Church of the Resurrection each Sunday. I recall, for the first time in my young life, listening to another child's fears and loneliness. Clarence and I often stood for a half hour or so on the street corner continuing our precious conversation about the feelings and meaning of the events that were sweeping over our lives and propelling us to a new future. We hated to part and go our separate ways home.

All of us, surprisingly, graduated from Grade 8 at Earl Haig Public School. In our honour, the Home and School Club hosted a dinner in the school's kindergarten room, the only place without desks bolted to the floor. The guest speaker for the occasion was Syl Apps, captain of our Toronto Maple Leafs. While we had been given the message of our generational importance many times over, the same message coming from our hockey hero Syl Apps possessed real meaning. Let there be no doubt, we were the hope for Canada's future and we had an important and large task ahead of us in rebuilding a better Canada. One entire generation had been condemned to sacrifice itself physically and financially, and now it was up to us to carry the torch of hope forward. It was heady stuff for 13- and 14-year-olds who had been observers of the world events during the 1940s. Syl Apps's words were not empty rhetoric to any of us as we listened intently to our hockey hero. Today young people are viewed less as assets in Canadian society and more as economic liabilities, but let me not get ahead of myself.

Childhood had its sunny moments as well. Every summer my parents would rent a small cottage for a week or two on a lake in Haliburton or Muskoka. In the early days we travelled north by train and later by bus. There was always considerable discussion in advance as to whether we could afford such a luxury, but my father's joy at being by a lake, taking long walks while smoking a White Owl cigar and having a nap when he felt like it was sufficient return on the investment. My mother, who always complained about the amount of work involved in getting ready for these vacations, recognized the significance of the annual break to my father's spirit.

Likewise, Christmas was always a time of warm family celebration. We always had a real tree, whose needles began falling on the family presents well before December 25. As a child I recall wondering whether it would be bare by Christmas morning. There was always an orange in the toe of my stocking, which hung at the foot of my bed, our house not having a fireplace. Even during the war years when tropical fruit was almost impossible to find or too expensive to purchase, Santa always brought me an orange. Whenever I smell a fresh orange today, warm memories of crawling to the foot of the bed in the dark and probing the mysterious shapes protruding from my Toronto Maple Leafs blue-and-white hockey stocking come flooding back. Proust has nothing on me when it comes to memories prompted by the smell of an orange.

I was an adventurous boy. On family walks as a toddler, I am told, I could never walk in a straight line from our home to the grocery store on Danforth Avenue. If my mother was not looking, I would scurry off into a laneway or up a narrow alleyway between the houses. At age four I climbed out of my backyard and headed to Monarch Park and the local clay quarry where they made bricks. No doubt I wanted to try out my new Sisman Scampers, which my mother had just purchased for me for $8. Somehow I managed to navigate the steep sides of the quarry so that I could get to the murky pond that lay nestled in the willows at the foot of the cliffs. I walked out on a protruding log so as to get a good view of the water, and then disaster struck. I slipped and fell into the pond. Fortunately the water was only up to my waist, but the clay on the bottom captured my feet. As I struggled back onto the log, one of my brand-new Sisman Scampers came off; the other, which was still on my foot, was covered with grey mud.

A few minutes later my mother, who had managed to get the quarry foreman to suspend blasting, rushed to my assistance with a couple of quarry workers in tow. Then the worst of all phrases was uttered: "Wait until your father gets home from work." Time has erased the memory of the spanking, but for years the single Sisman Scamper sat caked with dry mud above my father's workbench in the basement. It remained a visible symbol of my errant ways long into my youth, when my wanderings would eventually find more acceptable expression in the form of canoe trips and hiking. What sticks with me about this incident is not the extreme danger I was in, but rather the loss of my new shoe — shoes that had cost about 20 percent of my dad's weekly salary. I never had any doubts that I had committed a cardinal sin by losing that shoe.

As a child I didn't know that we were poor. Sure, we didn't have a car or a telephone until my early teens. We were also one of the last families in the neigbourhood to purchase a television set. We did, however, have a comfortable home, nutritious food on the table, adequate warm clothing and a lot of love. Once, I recall, we even ate at a local restaurant for some special occasion. I can't remember the occasion, but I had roast of lamb with mint sauce.

Perhaps the things that saved our family and the other families in our neighbourhood from falling into the culture of poverty, as distinct from the economic poverty in which we lived, was the strong sense of pride we all possessed. We were, through frugal budgeting, able to be independent and self-sufficient. We did not have to rely on charity or welfare to sustain ourselves. Sure, things could go wrong, and they did occasionally, but we had the feeling that we could pull in our belts one more notch and weather the situation. Those few people in the neighbourhood who had to go on welfare or resort to unemployment insurance felt deeply ashamed of their situations and moved heaven and earth to regain their financial independence. I later came to realize that the personal imperative of self-respect served as a built-in social control mechanism, keeping the early years of the welfare state a self-regulating system. The principles of benefit entitlement and universality reduced the sense of personal shame. While at some level this was a good thing, growing general greed overcame the founding reason for the social-welfare system. The social programs of the Canadian welfare state were intended and designed to serve as a safety net to be used in exceptional personal and family circumstances. Once this principle was lost we began to run into trouble.

The experience of the Great Depression and the deprivations of the war years surrounded those of us born during the period. It was by no means a comfortable culture. As I've pointed out several times, anxiety pervaded even the smallest acts. It did, however, make us a cohesive community and when someone took ill, neighbours were there to support the family. A death in the neighbourhood, no matter how distant the person, resulted in a door-to-door collection to raise enough money for a floral tribute to be sent from "the neighbours with sympathy." God forbid that you should die and have only two or three floral tributes surrounding your coffin.

When I was 16 years of age and my brother Bruce was five, my father lost his job. The owner of the small lawn bowl manufacturing shop died and the business was sold. Dad received $200 as severance pay and a letter of recommendation. The Unemployment Insurance Program, introduced in 1941, should have kicked in, but the settlement prevented this. For six months we had no other source of income, Mom having left her job in the greeting card company soon after war ended. I was in Grade 11 at Riverdale Collegiate Institute at the time, one of only three students from our local elementary school who did not go on to either Danforth Technical School or Eastern High School of Commerce. Immediately our modest lifestyle dropped several notches and the weekly Sunday roast gave way to overcooked liver or stew. I recall mother purchasing two pairs of heavy wool trousers for me to wear to school. By the time I had walked the three miles to school and three miles back during the first warm days of spring, the insides of my thighs were chafed almost raw by the coarse wool. There was no money to purchase lighter-weight trousers, so I endured by coating my legs with Vaseline. For the first time in my life I felt poor.

That summer I had been planning for our first canoe trip with my close childhood friend Jack Davidson and his bachelor uncle, Ernie. With only six weeks to go before departure on this dream-of-a-lifetime adventure, I cancelled my plans, realizing that I had to work full time during the summer to purchase my school books for the fall and to buy new pants. I went to work for the Broadview YMCA's day camp, Camp Etoby. Seven nights a week I also worked from 7:00 p.m. to 10:30 or 11:00 p.m. at Coxwell Stadium, attending to the baseball scoreboard for the East Toronto Women's Softball League. Despite this setback in my summer plans for a wilderness adventure, I kept the goal very much alive. I was to learn something else that critical summer — that I enjoyed working with children; in fact, I was pretty good at it.

Watching the weariness of my dad after a futile day's job search was even more painful than watching him return worn out from a day unloading cargo as a temporary stevedore on the Toronto docks. At least he had a brown pay envelope for his efforts on the docks and a little self-respect. There was also the day he came home with a large box of 48 Neilson chocolate bars wrapped in newspaper, one corner of which was mildly crushed. "Damaged during shipment," he said with a twinkle in his eyes. He handed the box to us and watched the smiles glow on our faces. It had been a long time since even the smallest luxury had come through the door.

By fall Dad was once again employed. He joined the maintenance staff of East General Hospital where he worked as a carpenter until his retirement. Despite the fact that he took a drop in salary, he was pleased to be working and contributing to his family once again. When school started in September, I went to Riverdale in a new pair of blue jeans, a little stiff but not made of sandpaper.

The summer of 1953 marked a turning of the tide in my relatively carefree life as a child. For the first time in my life (save for a couple of years when I made bicycle deliveries for Easton and Myers Drug Store on Saturday afternoons for 25¢ an hour) I held a responsible, full-time job as a day-camp counsellor. In fact, I held two jobs. By the end of the summer I had earned $240, a princely sum when your father never earned more than $35 a week. What was more impressive in my young life was how close to the edge we had come as a family as a result of Dad's unemployment. Modest though our existence was, I had always felt secure, perhaps lulled by the labour demands of the war years with its six-day week and constant overtime. Any visible expression of concern over our security was kept from me, leaving only a few disjointed incidents and an unspoken atmosphere of chronic worry as hints of our real financial circumstances.

Unemployment now had real meaning. Being only two years away from high school graduation, I was forced to think seriously for the first time about my future. Adventure had always been high on my priority list. Our brief summer forays to cottages on lakes in the Canadian Shield suggested to me that life as a forest ranger seemed like a good idea, though as I found out from further investigation, the job would require a degree in forestry if I wanted to seriously consider the option.

The family circumstances of the summer of 1953 pushed the possibility of four years at the University of Toronto following high school beyond any reasonable realm of financial possibility. Besides, the distractions of adolescence had all but buried the flicker of intellectual curiosity that had carried me into the collegiate stream of schooling.

Mediocre grades and a guidance counsellor from an old Rosedale family who seemed determined to keep us in our proper social station disconnected the last tenuous threads linking me to my childhood dream: "You should think seriously about getting a job once you graduate from high school. You obviously don't have the stuff to seriously consider university." Certainly my feeble grades were visible evidence of my weak potential, but burning somewhere in my psyche was the ember of stubborn determination which would eventually rekindle my childhood curiosity about ideas and things. All that daydreaming about grand adventures and a better life would not be wasted.

As a young child I had studied my dad's callused hands when he took me on his lap after dinner each night to read me "The Adventures of Uncle Wigley" from the *Toronto Telegram*. I had also felt the tingle of enthusiasm in his voice as he spoke about faraway places from the pictures contained in a collection of adventure books, which sat in three neat rows within the highly polished glass-fronted bookcase. The bookcase was the closest thing to a household shrine contained in our tiny Rhodes Avenue living room. There were three sets of hard-covered books, one blue, one grey and one red. I recall the respect with which the bookcase was opened and the book gently slid from its designated spot. I had to wash my hands before I could turn the pages while I sat beside my dad. The smell of rubber and perspiration in his work clothes accompanied us into the realm of exotic animals and faraway places. During my youth I began to realize that this man, my father, would have been a great adventurer had the Depression and the arrival of the family not distracted him from the course of his dream. As it was, we entered the larger world through these precious books, salvaged, I later found out, from the lending library section of a small cigar store on Danforth Avenue that he once owned before it went bankrupt.

When I visit Rhodes Avenue I still take pleasure in opening the bookcase, its veneer and window polished to a high gloss. Then I take out one of the books, having been sure to wash my hands. In a moment I'm transported to those faraway lands I shared with my father. In later years, while travelling to places such as Kairouan, Bukhara and Tbilisi, I thought to myself, "My God, these places do exist." How my father would have enjoyed being there.

Despite my uninspiring grades, I sensed that books and dreams, rather than tools and manual skills, deserved my attention. With my father's unemployment threatening our family that summer of 1953, I concluded that the surest route to breaking with the fragile security of the Couchmans' working-class heritage was to become a teacher. As far as I knew, I would be the first Couchman to choose a profession rather than a manual vocation. Besides, the doggie doorstop with the pointed head, for which I received a humble 6.5 grade out of 10 in manual training, suggested that I would never achieve my father's level of competency. That doorstop, by the way, still occupies a place of honour on a shelf in my home. I was also coming to realize that I found something remarkably satisfying about working with children. The first eddies of adulthood were beginning to swirl into the idle currents of my childhood.

That fall I joined the gentlemen and boys of St. Simon's Choir led by the formidable Eric Lewis. St. Simon's Anglican Church served the parish of Rosedale and a small portion of upper Cabbagetown, the latter area being quite similar to my own east Toronto neighbourhood. Eric Lewis, the son of a British civil servant from colonial India, was more traditionally British than any Englishman would ever care to be. Among his many ambitions, he had long made it a point to scout out musical talent from the other side of the tracks. This allowed him to achieve a mix of social classes within the choir, unbalanced though it always seemed to be. I realized, as I got to know this benevolent little tyrant of a man, that he possessed a personal agenda very much akin to Shaw's Professor Higgins. Through spit and polish he seemed determined to transform a few rough diamonds from Cabbagetown and east of the Don Valley into refined young men with both the social graces and expectations of our Rosedale-bred colleagues. Thus, St. Simon's Choir was not only possibly the best church choir in Canada, it was also a laboratory for Eric Lewis's unique style of social engineering. The image of the mortar and pestle is what comes to mind as I think of the grinding, authoritarian approach he employed to jar us from our rough, unrefined ways.

For the first time in my life, as a "young gentleman" of the choir, I realized there were homes that contained whole rooms of leather-bound books. And around the Sunday evening dinner table, everyone properly attired, conversations were considered a form of intellectual art. More to the point, I realized that most of the young men ahead of me in the choir were enrolled in Trinity College at the University of Toronto.

Unlike today, when it is so easy to glimpse the lives of the various social classes through television and high-powered advertising, I had little idea of who were "haves" and who were "have-nots" in my teen world of the 1950s. St. Simon's thus opened my eyes to a world so foreign to me that I could well have been in another country.

For the first time in my life I felt incredibly uncomfortable, as well as an unfocused sense of shame. Surrounding me was a force of authority that defined the way proper life should be led and reflected rigid confidence in the social order. There were, of course, values I recognized, such as doing one's duty, working hard and being honest. What was new to me, however, was the unquestioned sense of privilege that permeated all aspects of old, upper-class Anglo-Saxon culture of the mid-20th century in Canada.

On one summer occasion I met a particularly striking young woman at a choir picnic on someone's estate north of Toronto. She was one of the choirboy's sisters and was assisting with the games, as I was assigned to supervise. After considerable mental fumbling I rallied the courage to invite her out that coming Saturday evening, perhaps to take in a movie. Kilby responded with confident enthusiasm to the invitation and suggested that rather than a movie, why didn't we go the dance at the Royal Canadian Yacht Club? When I arrived at Kilby's Rosedale home on Saturday evening, having walked from the bus stop, I grasped the large brass knocker and allowed it to clunk once, creating an echoing thud. A servant responded and invited me to wait in the conservatory, a room with a large grand piano and marble floor, as I recall. Looking around, I calculated that the floor space was easily as large as our ground floor.

Later in the evening during the dinner accompanying the dance, I was seated at a table with several other young people my own age. Being on my best manners, I was astounded when one young man, the son of Jack Kent Cook, proceeded to pile cups and saucers into a giant leaning tower. Suddenly it came crashing down, scattering broken pieces of china all over the table and verandah of the elegant RCYC. When a waiter rushed over to the table there was absolutely no rebuke. "Oh dear, I see we've had an accident. I'll go and get a broom and sweep it up," said the waiter. The young architect of the tower responded, "Just put it on my father's bill."

"What an asshole," I muttered to myself as the other young people laughed nervously at the episode. I wondered on the drive home just how much cleaning up was done on behalf of characters such as this young man, particularly when they go on to design or run systems bigger than a pile of cups and saucers.

There were times when I found the entire social leap excruciatingly painful, so much so that I made efforts to leave the choir and withdraw from Eric Lewis's little experiment in social engineering. Eric seemed acutely aware of my fading motivation. He would always interject warm words of support, giving tangible recognition of my emerging new young adult self. He provided free music lessons, placed me a few seats closer to the soloist in the baritone section and ultimately made me his assistant in looking after the choirboys. Like Eliza Doolittle's dilemma, it was hard to shake free from the generosity of this benevolent little autocrat.

After fumbling my way through Grade 12 at Riverdale, I entered the Toronto Teacher's College two-year training program for non-honour diploma students. I had finally found a focus for my vocational and intellectual interests. I was to become an elementary school teacher and I would be a good one. I went at my education and recreational activities with a vengeance. On top of my studies at Toronto Teacher's College, I turned my summer YMCA work into a part-time job as a youth worker and locker room clerk and, of course, I pursued my choral and choir supervision work at St. Simon's on Friday evenings and Sundays. Every available minute was packed with activities designed to extricate me from the lethargy of simply hanging out on the corners of the east Toronto teen scene.

It was at this time that I met a friend who was to stir my moribund mind and arouse my lifelong commitment to social reform. I met George Richards at Broadview YMCA. George was my age and a recent immigrant from the slums of Glasgow. In retrospect, even with the balanced perspective that comes with age, George Richards came as close to being a genius as anyone I ever met in my life. It was George who opened my mind to the great philosophers, thinkers and mathematicians. He also possessed an impressive collection of classical records and we would spend hours listening to Beethoven, Mahler, Stravinsky and Bartok. We also engaged in lengthy political, religious and psychological discussions on the nature of society and our purpose in the world.

In Glasgow George had been plucked from the slums by the education system and sent to an elite academy for gifted students. Just before his father, a porter on ocean liners, decided to move the family to Toronto, George had graduated from the academy, obtaining firsts in every subject but French, where he scored second in his class. Coming from similar social roots, we saw ourselves as rebels in an unjust society. George, however, festered with resentment and anger against society and its institutions, while I saw these institutions as being my opportunity to secure both the education and tickets I required to pursue social justice from within the system.

We argued at length about the relative merits of these divergent approaches. George gradually withdrew from society, following the course of the intellectual beatniks of the early 1950s, while I, in contrast, began my fight from within the system. For several years we tolerated one another's different courses as we continued our dialogue and worked together with troubled youth from the east Toronto community. In the end, however, George became convinced that I had sold out my original values with respect to the social revolution, and we quietly and sadly went our separate ways.

One night, some 15 years later, I received a call at 12:30 a.m., George's usual calling time when we were close friends. I could hear the sound of Mahler in the background, some distant traffic noise and breathing. Despite my efforts to engage the caller, there was no response. He simply hung up. The next day I learned that George had died a lonely, unemployed alcoholic. Friends at the funeral all mentioned receiving the same silent goodbye call. I wept at the loss of a dear friend. Our paths had crossed and fused at a critical coming of age and then sadly parted. In his own unique and tragic way, George too was a victim of poverty.

Chapter 3

Out of the Streets
and
into the World

In September 1957 I began teaching Grade 5 at the Ionview Public School in Scarborough, Ontario. I was finally in my element and thoroughly enjoying the experience. In addition, I was being paid the princely sum of $2,800 per year, with promise of annual increments. By the following year I was earning more than my father in his job as carpenter at the East General Hospital. I also, through a special-entry program for teachers, entered a summer school program at Queen's University. In eight years I would obtain my B.A. degree, majoring in philosophy with a minor in psychology.

By the end of my second year teaching I was beginning to feel comfortable and confident in my work with children. One day I was approached by the school superintendent asking me whether or not I would accept student teachers, many of whom would be older and better trained than I was. In looking back at that era of rapid school growth, large classes and teaching colleagues whose average age was in the mid-20s, I am amazed that the generation of the baby boomers did so well under our meagre scholarly tutelage.

In 1960 I made my second major consumer purchase. The first was an electronic hi-fi console and three classical LP recordings. The console, as I recall, was a much better piece of furniture than a sound machine. A green Volkswagen was followed almost immediately by a green 16-foot Peterborough canoe. I could now get to my beautiful Algonquin lakes and take off into the wilderness on my own terms whenever I felt the longing, which was frequently. Good music and the freedom to travel. I felt like a very rich man.

My work as a teacher and as a YMCA youth leader was also beginning to attract attention. In 1960 I was invited to join the board of directors of Broadview YMCA, largely a local group of business leaders and merchants who operated factories and stores in east Toronto.

Soon after this dubious honour I received a call from Glen Drover, the Y's boys' work secretary, to meet with him and Tony Barclay, the local juvenile probation officer. Glen, who was considered somewhat of an intellectual, would later go on to become chair of the social work department at the University of British Columbia. The topic for discussion was an east end street gang of teens, all of whom were either on probation or serving time in Bowmanville Training School. Tony had tried breaking the group up by enrolling some of them in Scouts, some in the Y and others at local community centres. Within weeks, if not days, they would be thrown out of the programs and be back on the streets where they would terrorize the neighbourhood. I was asked if I would take the gang on as a detached youth worker. The approach had been utilized with some success in New York, under the auspices of the city's youth board. Rather than attempt to bring the gangs into the YMCA, where they would certainly cause trouble, I would work with them on the streets, laneways and hangouts of my east Toronto neighbourhood, where I still lived. The challenge was an exciting one, particularly as I was a full-time teacher, heavily involved at St. Simon's and working on my degree at Queen's.

During the next six years I was to become very close to my boys until, as with most older adolescents, they left school and discovered girls. Aside from learning a great deal more about human nature, the culture of severe poverty and families with far more difficulties than my own, we also made some progress at rehabilitating the boys. When I first met them in the basement of a Mennonite church across from the old Woodbine Race Track, they had an enviable record in their social circle.

They had 89 individual charges and had committed acts of vandalism totalling $189,000. Over the first three years of my work with them, only nine charges were laid against them and vandalism damage was reduced to around $12,000, most of it a result of a single act of window smashing at the local Coca-Cola bottling plant.

I had two approaches in my limited group-work repertoire, the first being to work at influencing the gang's natural leadership, which consisted of Tom and his two lieutenants, Jim and Barton, a Métis lad from Manitoulin Island. Trying to work against this trio was an impossible task. Secondly, I altered the setting as much as possible by taking them hiking and camping to my favourite haunts. Outside their urban turf they found themselves in a foreign land. I recall comforting one 17-year-old around a campfire one evening. His fear of the dark and the silence had moved him to tears. On another occasion Barton, who was three inches taller than I and outweighed me by 20 pounds, confided that what he liked most about life "is walking in the forest and looking at all the beautiful spring flowers," adding, "and if you tell anyone I told you this, I'll smash your head in." Late in my career I was to see this approach utilized by Outward Bound in their Youth Challenge program, as well as with physically and sexually abused women in the Women of Courage program. I was pleased to have a role in launching both of these programs. As with my detached street work, I developed a sense that there might be better ways to reach people than through conventional therapeutic programs. Innovation thrilled me with its challenges.

My innovative approach to social work practice through my work with street gangs soon came to the attention of education and social services leaders. In the early 1960s officials had become quite concerned with Ontario's high school drop out rate. A major conference was scheduled by the Metro Toronto Social Planning Council to be held at Geneva Park, and I was asked to make a presentation on my detached youth work with the Broadview YMCA.

This conference was to be my first real contact with the social-service system and the professional psychiatrists, social workers, psychologists, educators and policy analysts with whom I would come to work in the years ahead. Up till then my discussions on such matters had always been with my friend and fellow Y youth worker George Richards, with a little rambling supervision from Glen Drover and Tony

Barclay, my boys' probation officer. None of these discussions had prepared me for the professional proceedings of the Geneva Park conference. Suddenly Tom, Jim, Barton, Ron, David, Brian and the rest of my gang of spirited urban pirates were coded and classified as multi-problemed, emotionally disturbed and socially alienated adolescents. On the other hand, my work with the boys was heralded as a "highly innovative intervention" and I was suddenly catapulted to the outer margins of the social-service system. It didn't dawn on me at the time, however, that the small pilot youth-work programs of that period were to remain modest gestures toward innovation and social-service change on the part of the system. This was the first hint that organizations and systems tend to resist change.

I can recall being invited by the YMCA to speak at the annual meeting about our street-work program and being showered with accolades. A week later when I asked whether I could bring the boys in for a swim, I was told that it would be better to keep my boys outside the building, given the havoc that two or three of them had wreaked on the Y's programs and facilities when Tony Barclay had initially attempted to enroll them in the YMCA. There was also, of course, no money to cover program expenses or any salary for my work, though the latter didn't trouble me particularly, as I had income from my day job as a teacher. To cover travel costs, food and equipment expenses, I was left to my own devices to raise funds. Thankfully, the East Toronto Optimists Club came to my rescue, and for six years it provided our operating expenses. Throughout the program's life span, all income was self-generated. Not only did I work out in the streets and laneways of east Toronto, but I also worked outside the normal support framework of the organization that officially sponsored the YMCA's detached youth-worker program. Not until the mid-1960s was Grant Lowery finally hired by the YMCA to oversee support and supervision to detached youth-work services.

At the time my work with the boys seemed simply to be the right thing to do. Here was a group of kids who needed a helping hand and I had the interest and a few skills to assist them. Until I met the professionals at the Geneva Park conference on unreached youth, it never dawned on me that there was a major industry dedicated to studying and flittering about the service margins of my boys and their so-called multi-problem families. With the crumbling of the 1940s and

1950s culture of self-sufficiency and duty, this latent industry of professional caregivers would begin to supplant voluntary effort such as my own. Social workers, psychologists, psychiatrists and other experts were to happily take on social responsibility and obligations that for centuries had been the almost exclusive domain of family, friends and neighbours, with occasional help from the church and fraternal organizations.

One of the consequences of my growing profile was being chosen by the YMCA to represent the North American delegation to the organization's Young Adult Conference in Vienna. Not only was this my first trip outside Canada (save for going to Buffalo to see a vaudeville show, an initiation right for up-and-coming east Toronto young men) but I was to lead a large delegation of my peers. This was also, at age 24, my first airplane flight. I recall we crossed the Atlantic on a BOAC Bristol Britannia. I thanked God for Eric Lewis's ministrations at St. Simon's. I had to attend official receptions in palaces once owned by Hungarian aristocracy, concerts by the Vienna Philharmonic and speeches to delegates from around the world. For a young person from east Toronto, caviar, champagne and international issues were a heady mix.

Following Vienna we went on to Prague and the towns of Czechoslovakia, which were still in the grip of Stalinism, despite its fall from grace in Khrushchev's new Soviet Union. It was an amazing time to visit this beautiful country, as it had only opened its doors to Western tourism the year before. It was by no means a happy place, though some of the country's poor appreciated the simple luxuries of the new era. One elderly woman travelling in our compartment on the train put it very simply: "Before communism we had no peach melba; now we have peach melba." I could relate to this. That night we sat down to boiled cabbage and horse meat in a dingy Prague restaurant. I could find no peach melba on the menu.

With each passing year new doors were opening for me. I was beginning to see the world as an amazing place, full of complexities and challenges. None of these could I quite understand, but they excited me. In many ways it was like straying into that clay pit when I was four years of age, an equally dangerous venture that demanded risks, but whose challenges stimulated my curiosity.

When my first street work project completed its course, I was asked by the professional establishment how I would judge its success.

First of all, no one in the mid-1960s took such evaluative judgments of social programs very seriously, nor did anyone have the instruments to conduct a careful analysis of new program initiatives. We were superb at describing our efforts but could only provide the crudest of evaluative measures. An incident occurred a year or two later that caused me to pause and think about what my six years with the boys had accomplished.

Jim and Barton, the gang's two lieutenants, had got themselves into trouble and ended up in jail as young adults. One day they seized the opportunity to walk away from the minimum-security provincial reformatory where they were serving 18-month terms. During the days that followed they broke into a house and, along with clothes and $6,000 in cash, they stole the owner's handgun. When I became aware (through the grapevine) that they were armed, I notified the police. Shortly afterward they were confronted by police in a service station as they were filling the tank of their stolen car. They bolted from the scene on foot and forced their way into a doctor's home, holding the doctor's wife and two small children as hostages. The police immediately surrounded the house and ordered them to throw out their gun and come out through the front door with their hands in the air. In a surprise move Barton grabbed the gun from Jimmy and threw it out the window. "What the fuck are you doing?" shouted Jimmy, the smaller of the two. "Come on, let's do what they're asking," said Barton, and out the door they went with a little physical aid from Barton.

When I later spoke to Barton in Collin's Bay Penitentiary about this hair-raising incident, I asked him why he had been so spontaneous in following the police's instructions. He said that the little girl in the family had reminded him of my daughter Barbara. "She was frightened and in tears. I didn't want to scare her, so I figured I'd grab the gun and throw it out the window."

After hearing this story I realized that measures of success are highly relative. I also began to appreciate that a program's ultimate success may have little bearing on whether organizations choose to continue or expand such programs. In terms of my work with the boys, we had our setbacks, as the above story indicates. On the whole, however, my urban pirates settled down to more or less normal lives. The gang's leader, Tom, became an early computer programmer. Jim, the reluctant desperado, is now the service manager of a large automotive store. He's married with children and has a Winnebago in his suburban driveway. I've lost track of Barton but I have no doubt that one of these days I'll come across him in the mountains one spring, when the lupines, crocuses and anemones are in bloom. "And if you tell anyone I told you this, I'll smash you in the head."

One thing I understood from this incident was the difficulty of measuring success. I was soon to find that all future efforts would be judged against rigorous standards of financial accountability. However, measuring effectiveness was a much more challenging matter. Now I realize that being able to determine whether a program is actually helping people is the most critical side of the equation. I was to see, however, in the coming years that financial accountability would be the dominant indicator of success. Effectiveness would be measured by crude instruments. How many boys were in my street gang, how many attended our gatherings, how many hours did I put in and how many kids ended up back in reformatory? More and more, my work would be judged by productivity indicators, not true effectiveness.

In 1963, on the wave of my growing profile in dealing with troubled kids, I left my teaching job in Scarborough to become head of student services for the Etobicoke Board of Education. In that final year at Ionview Public School I had been assigned 42 Grade 8 students. Halfway through the year a clique of three particularly disruptive youngsters was added to my 12- and 13-year-old baby boomers, in order to offer some relief to my university-trained colleague down the hall. His enrollment dropped to 37 Grade 8 students. Meanwhile, I was literally pinned to the blackboard by the additional desks. One day it occurred to me that if I had a knack of reaching kids who were "challenging," as the principal described them to me, perhaps I should find a job where I could pursue my exclusive talent full time. At 26 years of age, with more enthusiasm then clinical skill, I took on my new assignment in Etobicoke.

Because of the unique nature of my new job, which was dreamed up by Jack Stinson, Etobicoke's superintendent of special education, I had to undergo an interview with Ken Pruder and Tom Boone, the board's co-directors of education. They were somewhat baffled by Jack's vision of my free-floating role. After explaining how I would work, a somewhat modified version of my detached street worker role, the director of education asked me what I would do if I found myself trapped in a basement apartment with a 200-pound angry father who had long-standing grievances with the schools. No doubt the director was mildly concerned with my modest 140-pound physique. "As long as I can get my mouth open before he decides to throw a punch, I should be all right," I responded. Throughout the rest of my career I found I could get myself out of numerous jams so long as I could talk before all hell broke loose.

Day One of my new job met all my expectations. "Come and see Ryan," said the principal at Queensway Public School. "He's back in the school after stabbing another lad in the back during a fight last spring." Later the same September morning a call came from another school, suggesting that a well-to-do family in the community was keeping a psychotic 12-year-old boy locked in their attic. It turned out in this situation that the boy's mother had seized her son from a state psychiatric hospital in New York and driven him to her parents' home on Etobicoke's exclusive Kingsway Drive. Finally, a call came in from a school in a public housing neighbourhood. The principal was nursing a badly bruised shin after an eight-year-old, new to the school that day, had kicked him and then run home. Late that afternoon after several relatively minor calls, I drove to the Fairlawn basement apartment of the young recalcitrant. Somewhere in my limited training, perhaps it was Psychology 101 at Queen's, I had learned enough to know that a professional should take a social history of the child. After asking all the obvious questions about what might be troubling the wee lad, I asked the boy's mother, "Does your son suffer from enuresis?"

"What's that?" she replied.

"Does he pee the bed?"

"Yeah," Frank's mother responded, "but so did his dad until we got married. I soon put a stop to that, however."

Certainly my work was not without its lighter moments. However, the tragedy of lives unrealized and the pain, which was all too evident, moved me greatly. These situations and the many others to follow touched the chord of obligation in my spirit. I was certainly no saint, but perhaps I could make life a little easier for a few people. While I didn't realize it at the time, that woman cutting out those cardboard soles and the child giving her shoes away to a child in greater need were images that would haunt my life.

The boy who had stabbed another in the back, the frightened child who kicked the principal's shins and the mysterious boy in the attic were but a small sample of the thousands of youngsters my staff and I would see over the next 11 years I would serve in Etobicoke. I had been pushed up against the blackboard by my 45 Grade 8 students in Scarborough. Now the demands of 60,000 students would keep me pinned against the wall for several years to come. Jack Stinson, my boss, was an intuitive and compassionate man who sensed that we were doing something very right. As a former athlete who had had considerable success reaching troubled and delinquent kids through sports and direct conversations, he placed absolute trust in my work. He was also magnificent at running interference with the upper echelons of Etobicoke's administration on those thankfully rare occasions when someone began to feel we were stepping beyond our specific Ministry of Education mandate. Of course, we were, but it was making a difference and Jack and I both knew it.

This was my first experience working within the bureaucracy of the system. It was also the first time in my life, aside from intellectual exchanges with George on being, nothingness and the self-interest of capitalism, that I began to seek an overview on how our community, government services, professional elites and institutions function. From the vantage point of someone who had been raised outside the community of privilege and influence, who had been assigned to work on the streets and was now on the perimeter of the education establishment, I was struck by the incredible effort required to bring simple, rational order to human elements, which are complex, emotionally charged, often ugly and very much interrelated to one another. The system, however, took these people and neighbourhood cultures and would divide their needs into health, education, recreation and social requirements. Professionals would then be trained to address each separate need using a language specific to their discipline.

I was suddenly jolted into recognizing this phenomenon at one of those classic case conferences that were so popular among professionals in the 1960s. Ten individuals representing education, mental health, child welfare corrections and the welfare department were called together for a two-hour conference to discuss John, a 10-year-old boy and his family of six. Because of the seriousness of the child's difficulties, several agencies sent a supervisor in addition to a social worker or teacher. After the initial round of introductions we soon became aware that each agency was investing between four and 140 hours a month working with John and his family. Despite this effort he was steadily deteriorating. At a critical juncture in the complex discussion on what was really wrong with Johnny and who was doing what about it, Ned McKeown of the Toronto Board of Education looked around the room. In his frustration, Ned announced that for half the funds being spent on John and his family he could provide the child with his own exclusive special-education teacher and a full-time homemaker could be assigned to the family. "I have no doubt," said Ned, "that this would improve the lad's situation." Everyone knew Ned was correct but no one had the professional courage to challenge the system so that the right thing could be done. As a result, each of us covered ourselves in the prescribed professional manner and John's situation continued to worsen.

Absent at John's case conference were the informal caregivers from the community who were concerned about John and his family's well-being. There were no neighbours, youth workers, clergy or police officers, the people who lived daily with the family's problems. Having until recently been one such community support person, working with delinquent boys and their families, I was struck by how readily we, as professionals, overlooked these natural resources.

As noted earlier, Canada's new welfare-state programs seemed to me to be substituting trained professionals for the help of neighbours, friends and family. The shift from informal natural support systems was being justified on the basis that too many people had fallen through the gaps of the traditional system. What was needed was a universal social safety net run by well-trained professionals to ensure the social well-being of all citizens. As systemic rights guaranteed by the state became Canada's new social vision, personal duty and obligation began to fade as Canadian cultural values.

While it was quite unintentional, the consequence of professionalizing and regulating the care-giving systems was to denigrate the natural experience and skills of the family and community. The growth of professionalism also served to promote dependency on the part of many families. On the other hand, the growth of the professional social-service sector significantly diminished the hit-and-miss basis of informal systems of care and improved certain interventions, such as family counselling and the protection of abused and neglected children. If my neighbour Andrew's situation of abuse, mentioned earlier, were to occur today, I thought to myself, it would not be left solely to the kindly intervention of my mother. On the other hand, we were becoming too focused and overly dependent upon professionals to look after us.

Natural support systems, which often worked extremely well in supporting troubled or needy individuals and families, had suddenly become flawed and out of date in the minds of professionals and bureaucrats. What was even more critical in the change of cultural values was that social programs in Canada became a right for all people, rather than a service to be employed under exceptional circumstances, such as serious illness, job loss or disability. With the demise of the culture of personal duty and self-sufficiency came a new Canadian culture based upon rights and expectations.

In 1945 I recall a government cheque arriving in the mail each month for $6. This baby bonus money, made out to my mother, was eagerly welcomed. It was the first time the government had done anything tangible to help our struggling family, and I recall the genuine appreciation felt by my parents and their neighbours for this unsolicited assistance. It went immediately into buying clothes, shoes and other requirements, such as day camp at the Broadview Y. In 1962 after the birth of our daughter Barbara, my wife and I were taken aback when our first family allowance cheque arrived for a slightly larger amount. We really didn't need the money, but what the hell, it came out of our taxes so why not spend it. We stuck the money into a bank account for Barbara's university education. Just about every other family with kids in our middle-class circle of friends felt the same way about this largesse.

About this time another phenomenon of the system began to emerge in my consciousness. Both institutions and the social-service system seemed highly resistant to change. Little did I know at the time I first stumbled upon this seemingly obvious characteristic that it would become an issue that would haunt me throughout the remainder of my career and my life. Resistance to change was to become my vocational burden, sometimes overwhelming me, while at other times challenging my spirit and my intellect as I attempted to move institutions and systems off their inevitable track of self-serving perpetuity. I thought about Sisyphus being condemned to push his boulder up a hill only to have it roll down the other side. Then he would roll it back up only to see it roll once again to the base

43

of the hill. This he was condemned to do for eternity. I suspect that he would have viewed the task that a few of my colleagues and I were undertaking as a similar act of frustration. In search of a better opportunity to attack the problem, I accepted an offer to become the executive director of the Family Service Association (FSA) of Toronto. The year was 1974.

I knew a bit about FSA, having watched with interest a project launched by the agency, the Metro Toronto Children's Aid Society and the North York Board of Education in the late 1960s. This coalition undertook what is now called a "community development approach" in the low-income public housing project of Lawrence Heights. Within three short years the number of children coming into care was sharply reduced, as were the number of children requiring close monitoring by the Children's Aid Society's child protection workers. By pooling resources in a true collaboration, using the school as the neighbourhood's focal point for service, the community members responded with eagerness to the approach. They viewed the project as a means of looking after one another with the help of some talented professionals. After a couple of years the three agencies and the researchers monitoring the Lawrence Heights project declared it a real success.

At the time I was a board member of the CAS, so my role in supporting the initiative was minimal. Seeing its success, however, I was eager to see the Lawrence Heights project replicated in other high-density public housing communities in Metro Toronto. At a board meeting in 1969 the moment came to authorize the continuance of the Lawrence Heights project, as well as expand the model into three new housing developments. Moments before the vote was to be taken Ed Magder, the Ministry of Community and Social Services observer representative to the board, spoke: "I have been instructed by the ministry to advise you that you cannot spend further ministry funds on such projects. It would therefore not be advisable to vote in favour of this motion to expand the program any further."

There are few times during my career that I lost my cool; this was one of them. I was furious with the intervention and the remainder of the board was stunned. I shot back, "As an autonomous and independent board we have every right to make our own decisions on programs we feel are of benefit to the children in our care. We have a staff motion on the table recommending we expand the program and I, for one, am going to support it."

Ed Magder responded, addressing the chairman of the board, "If you vote in favour of this motion, Mr. Chairman, I'm afraid the ministry will have to withdraw its financial support in the amount required for the project's operation."

After further brief discussion the board voted against the motion, those responding to the ministry's threat defeating the motion by a four to one margin. Not only would the project not be expanded, but the current project was terminated. In my anger I responded by declaring that our board was no longer in charge of major policy issues but had become simply a citizen advisory committee to the ministry: "Under such circumstances, Mr. Chairman, we might as well turn the agency over to the government to run, as we no longer have effective policy control as a board of directors." While several colleagues said after the meeting it was a heroic defence, few people expressed any serious concern with the ministry's intervention. He who pays the piper calls the tune. It was as simple as that.

However, I thought about what had happened and it seemed to me that our emerging systems of human care, largely funded by government, were becoming autonomous little empires governed by civil servants and professional specialists. The Lawrence Heights project had broken an unspoken cardinal rule of the system. You don't mix affairs of the Ministry of Education with those of the Ministry of Community and Social Services or, for that matter, any other ministries concerned with the health, social well-being, education or recreation of people.

Each jurisdiction is a silo into which tax money is poured through the top and a specialized service comes out through a narrow spout at the bottom. Begin to mix the contents of the silos and you run the serious risk of losing accountability for the blended program. In government there seems nothing worse than losing track of accountability, even if it results in a marked improvement in outcomes.

Resistance to change is not always as blunt a weapon as the collapse of the Lawrence Heights initiative would suggest. In 1969 I was fortunate to acquire the assistance of Dr. Harvey Golombek with my small but growing student service department at the Etobicoke Board of Education. Harvey was a young psychiatrist, working in the child and adolescent department of the Clarke Institute of Psychiatry in Toronto. He had recently completed his training in Michigan as an adolescent specialist and was fascinated with the potential of community psychiatry for improving the general mental health of young people. Furthermore, Harvey was my age and shared the same enthusiasms as I did. Interestingly enough he came from a somewhat similar social background, having grown up in the Parkdale region of west central Toronto. We soon discovered we were kindred spirits.

One year into our new working relationship we began plotting how we might introduce a team approach to children's mental-health services in selected Etobicoke schools. Up to this point psychiatrists and psychologists going into schools were largely seen as the experts. A child displaying unusual behaviour or underperforming would be identified by the teacher, referred to the school psychologist or consulting psychiatrist, assessed, labelled and sent back to the teacher with a handy list of suggestions, many of which were difficult to implement by a teacher with 25 to 30 other children in the classroom. The psychologist or psychiatrist would then move on to another child or other school and rarely return to see how the child was doing. In a few instances where more in-depth treatment was seen as advisable, the child would be referred to a local mental-health agency in the community. After six months to a year the child would come to the top of a waiting list and be seen, usually for outpatient treatment. The system reminded me of automobile servicing. You sense that something is wrong with your car. You take it to a garage. A mechanic identifies what he thinks is the problem, fixes the car and gives it back to you. Teachers had a similar faith that once the experts had fixed the child, he or she would now be normal and would work diligently and behave properly.

Obviously children and their families are not cars, and while experts can be extremely helpful in assessing the nature of a child's difficulties, it takes the combined resources of the school, mental-health professionals, the family and often some other community social and recreational resources working closely together over time to help the child.

In our mental-health team approach we decided to place the classroom teacher at the centre of our team effort. After all, the teacher has the child approximately six hours each day, and no significant behavioural change can be effected by a psychologist or psychiatrist who may see the child for an hour a week for two to 10 weeks, which was the average length of treatment in the late 1960s. Also, a Ph.D. or medical degree does not assure success when it comes to helping children. We believed that behavioural change occurs only after relationships are firmly established, and a teacher has a much better chance of establishing a solid relationship with a child than a psychologist or psychiatrist. The teacher, however, can benefit from the professional's trained insights and requires continuing support from both colleagues and the family if he or she is to help the child. Our team approach was a radical departure from the rigid hierarchical treatment system of the day, which placed the classroom teacher at the bottom of the ladder. It was eminently sensible and, above all, it worked.

Within six months of beginning our first couple of pilot schools, we were receiving calls from other principals requesting that Harvey and I bring the program to their schools. At the end of Year One, 15 programs had been established and Harvey was recruiting residents in psychiatry from the University of Toronto, where he taught, to assist our efforts. Likewise, I recruited senior members of my student services department to help establish this new program.

So popular had the Etobicoke school mental-health team approach become that Harvey Golombek and I turned our energies toward publication of the work as well as presentations at education and psychiatric forums, such as the annual conference of the Canadian Psychiatric Association. As the program's profile grew, it became important to share the results of this successful venture with the trustees of the school board. Up to this point we had been keeping a low profile within the system and only responding to requests from elementary and secondary school principals who were genuinely eager to have a mental-health team in their schools. When the program was exposed to the trustees, however, they suddenly moved to make it official policy of the board. It was declared that every school within Etobicoke would be required to establish a school mental-health team within the year. At first Harvey and I were delighted with the clear success of our efforts. It soon became apparent, however, that this endorsement by the board was a mixed blessing.

Soon we began to receive requests from principals who were less than enthusiastic about establishing mental-health teams in their schools. As they put it, their job was educating children not delivering mental-health services. That was the job of the health-care system and should have no place in a school system. Within a few months we began to encounter our first failures. While the resistance was subtle due to the edict from the school trustees, it was just as forceful as any outright refusal to co-operate. It soon became apparent to us that our program was doomed by its very success. Whether it be a senior government bureaucrat flatly rejecting innovation or school principals subtly sabotaging a program of which they wanted no part, resistance to change is inherent within the systems our society has established to support children and their families.

At the same time as this was happening another revolutionary change was beginning to unravel the traditional intergenerational and institutional relationships. These relationships had kept Canadian society functioning in a relatively cohesive manner since I was a child. A generation raised in the aspirations of their parents' dreams for a more peaceful and materially comfortable world was beginning to attack the post-war social and economic order. The welfare state, intended to herald in an era of prosperity and personal security, was slowly being forced to alter its first principles, as both personal and professional self-interest were becoming dominant values within the late post-war culture of Canada.

Chapter 4

From the Trenches
to
the Ramparts

It happened innocuously enough. At the time none of us was even aware of the subtle shift in social values. As with most major social and cultural change in society, it happened at the local level and it manifested itself in the behaviour and attitudes of young people. Until well into the 1960s, no one could see that random changes in the behaviour of young people might represent a serious challenge to the authority and traditional values of post-war North American society.

I recall receiving a phone call one day from an irate principal of an Etobicoke secondary school. A 15-year-old boy had been temporarily suspended from school because he had "had the audacity to show up in class with hair that reached just below his collar line." While it was not uncommon in the mid- to late 1960s for school principals to force the issue of hair length, few principals went to the extreme of enacting suspension against a student. In this situation the boy had the support of his parents, who had gone to the press on the issue. He was now refusing to return to school unless he could do so on his own terms, which meant keeping his long hair. The principal had sent the vice-principal to the home to reason with the boy and his parents, but to no avail. To make matters even worse Max Ferguson of CBC's *Rawhide Show* had got hold of the incident and had created a skit of the situation. It was broadcast across the nation one quiet October afternoon. Of course, at this point the entire situation was being viewed as a major challenge to the ultimate authority of the entire school system. I agreed to meet with the boy and his parents in the principal's office to mediate the situation. After a few dignified words and some attention to the fundamental issue of the boy's education, the boy was readmitted to school. His hair remained below his collar but, in deference to the principal, it was to be kept clean and trim.

After a few similar calls I allowed my own hair to grow just below the collar length and began to sport a beard, which I kept neatly trimmed. This ended the calls and with many schools having accepted the new hairstyle from the outset, the few school principals who had forced the issue soon realized there were far more important matters to address, including the retention of students in school and the declining state of education.

Dramatic changes in styles within the popular culture are often symptomatic of more fundamental changes within society. Certainly hair length, which was precipitated by the North American invasion by the Beatles, heralded a shift in attitudes and values that would ulti- mately shake Western culture to its very core. Since 1929 the lives of the majority of people had been strictly governed by powerful external eco- nomic and political forces beyond the control of ordinary people. The Great Depression had dictated the basic survival strategies of my par- ents and grandparents. And before they had an opportunity to take con- trol of their lives in the early 1940s, the war years had heaped new and unforgiving burdens upon their tired shoulders. Such conditions fos- tered simple loyalties within families, modest material expectations and a respect for strong political and professional authority.

During the early years of the post-war economic revival there was a sense that good fortune would not last long. So conditioned were we by the adversity of 20 long years of struggle in protecting and restoring our very modest lives that nothing could be taken for granted. Furthermore, we were born to the belief that rigid social structure, firm gender-role definitions and the basic values of hard work, saving and being respon- sible were crucial to basic human survival. That you might actually enjoy life and be a little frivolous in your behaviour was tantamount to inviting a personal fall. Not until well into the 1950s, therefore, did the families and children of my parents' generation begin to lift their heads. Like most people who live too long in the survival mode, they couldn't really enjoy their rising good fortune. As in previous generations moulded by hardship, much of a family's hope is transferred to its children. The rising birthrate of post-war Canada was one of the very few hints of improving public confidence.

Baby boomers were born into the good life. Their parents were adamant that, unlike their own frustrated selves, their children would be safe and never have to suffer serious external disruptions to their lives. Pent up within the narrow human confines of lives moulded by deprivation and threats to security, however, were other elements of the human condition seeking emancipation. It should come as no surprise, therefore, that baby boomers would give visible expression to their parents' unconscious desires by challenging political, professional and institutional authority.

The most profound of all the acts of personal liberation, however, was the expression of sexual freedom, precipitated by the introduction of the birth control pill and the subsequent rise of feminism in the mid-1960s. More than any purely economic factor, the rise of feminism would change the social and economic fabric of all major Western societies in the final three decades of the century. On both a personal and professional level I experienced the surge of feminist emancipation as it swept over the male bastion of traditional gender beliefs and values. We were more than a little confused by events and the new order in our relationships with women.

Most surviving accounts of the late 1960s hippie revolution are written from the perspective of eager participants. Garlanded in psychedelic tie-dyed colours, the youth of the period would have you believe that they drifted through adolescence on rainbow clouds of love and uninhibited freedom, inspired by their own rebellion and the beat of their revolutionary music. While actual participants in the so-called hippie movement probably never exceeded five to 10 percent of young people, the culture they created was to have a very profound influence on the entire society. Like prior children's crusades, however, it was high on idealism and weak on attending to practical realities. It also had a dark side. Lacking the security and protection of family and community

institutions, the innocence of young people was easily exploited and frequently abused. Serious drug usage was the most identifiable problem
encountered by many of the young people, particularly when it shifted
to purely recreational use in the final years of the decade. The "drug
problem" was comfortably identified by the media and political authorities as the cause for all this rebellious behaviour in the nation's young
people. Lacking insight into the underlying reasons for such a major
social upheaval, drug abuse was the perfect simplistic explanation. It
shifted responsibility for the revolution off the shoulders of society's
institutions and families and placed it upon nebulous, dark external
forces. The drug pusher, standing in the shadows of a Yorkville or
Haight-Ashbury alley, thus became the arch villain of the era.

In the late winter of 1970 I received a phone call from the Hon. Tom
Wells, Ontario's minister of health. A group of social agency leaders in
Toronto, known as Project 69 and then Project 70, had been lobbying
government to take action on the increasingly serious problem of drug
abuse among teens, particularly among those young people associated
with the counterculture. A number of the members of the Project 69
and 70 group had been actively experimenting with non-traditional
street-level programs that allowed easy access for treatment and help.
Naturally I was familiar with these approaches and was intrigued to see
what progress had been made since I worked in this manner in the late
1950s and early 1960s. While it struck me as odd that the premier himself wanted to announce the establishment of the project in the legisla-
ture, I soon realized that the sons and daughters of many folks in the
so-called establishment had also been lobbying for such an initiative.

I immediately surrounded myself with highly capable and equally
enthusiastic research associates. We then hired 40 investigators at a cost
of $40 each per week and set them loose to interview counterculture
young people as well as the staff of hospitals, social agencies, school
boards and the police. One investigator, a young lawyer recently admit-
ted to the bar, came highly recommended as someone capable of pene-
trating the highest-level bureaucratic screens in order to uncover
information. Eddie Greenspan met all our expectations in this regard,
managing to secure interviews with senior officials with a maximum of
two days' notice. Several years later I ran into Eddie at the induction of
a mutual friend to the bench of the juvenile and family court. He
recalled the Project 70 study with much delight and jokingly noted that

the $40 we once paid him for a week's work would now buy only a few minutes of his time.

In many respects, the social crisis precipitated by the counterculture movement of the late 1960s and early 1970s was the golden age of social-service reform. Traditional approaches to care were overwhelmed by the cultural and political power of the movement. The majority of young people were, of course, by no means ill. They were, however, experiencing a major existential crisis of identity. The pent-up rebellion among youth that exploded in the late 1960s was the manifestation of 40 years of suppressed parental frustration and anger. Freedom of expression and personal hopes had been dashed by severe economic deprivation and by war. Only now, in the relative security of a booming economy, could a generation two decades removed from real physical and emotional hardship challenge the rigid social and political alignments that had allowed their parents and grandparents to survive the Great Depression and the subsequent war years.

No institution in society was more stressed by these circumstances than the family. In fact, as indicated earlier, many children of the establishment were actively involved in the movement. Thus, the youth counterculture revolution was no longer a remote social phenomenon. Such widespread rebellion by young people against the values and traditions of their families was difficult for parents of teenagers to understand and it hurt them deeply. These parents had grown up during the Great Depression and survived the war due to incredible self-discipline and focused determination. They had not enjoyed the luxury of a prolonged and relaxed adolescence, but rather had been rushed into premature adulthood with unquestioned values shoring up their psyches against anticipated hardship. Their driven sense of responsibility had allowed them, no, demanded of them, that they create a happier and more secure world for their children should personal and national economic circumstances ever permit. Ready access to higher education and the provision of financial security were to be their legacies to their children.

The response parents received for their efforts was baffling to most families. All those sacrifices, plus the music lessons, summer camp and driving to early-morning hockey practices must surely be appreciated by our young people. Under such circumstances, children should be grateful not rebellious. Watching their own suppressed frustration acted out with such complete and unrestrained abandon was overwhelming.

In an indirect way, the events of the late 1960s also radically changed the traditional nuclear family as we had known it. TV shows such as *Ozzie and Harriet*, *Father Knows Best* and *Leave It to Beaver* were suddenly out of fashion, while shows about single parents, dysfunctional families and singles were in. A new age of personal freedom and fulfillment began to sweep away the social structures of interdependence and responsibility, which had so long governed the behaviour of families to protect them against hardship and grief.

What is now interesting in retrospect, however, was the very strong sense of caring and sharing that you could feel all around you during this era. It was indeed an echo of the values of the 1930s and 1940s. Alas, most parents could not appreciate these values as expressed in their new form.

Society in post-war Canada had greatly valued social interdependence and social responsibility. As welfare programs were only to be used under exceptional circumstances of personal or family misfortune, the public responded positively to the concepts and principles of Leonard Marsh's Report on Social Security for Canada (1943). This was the federal report that provided the policy basis for the later introduction of Canada's welfare-state programs. The pioneers of Canada's social programs could not foresee the dramatic shift in fundamental cultural values. The very idea that self-fulfillment and personal rights would soon come to dominate the culture as moral principles was anathema to my parents' generation and to the public policy architects of their era. Though noble in intent, the desire to provide their children and grandchildren with a secure and materially comfortable world was to forcefully alter the cultural landscape. Thus, by the time many of the new programs were being introduced, a sense of entitlement, of one's personal rights, was beginning to usurp personal and collective responsibility as the dominant values of Canadian character. Under such social and moral conditions, universality, entitlement, professional self-interest and, inevitably, greed were to characterize Canadian culture and values. Like a virus seeded into the body awaiting the right conditions in the immune system to erupt, the new values would lie dormant in our social programs for almost two decades before erupting in the mid-1980s to fracture the entire system.

It was the hope of our Project 70 team, now that we had the close personal ear of Cabinet, that we could use the opportunity to challenge the evolution of children and youth services in the province. If ever there was a window of opportunity for institutional and systems reform, certainly the social turmoil of the period presented that opportunity. Already we had come to realize that agencies were reluctant to make significant changes when all was going well, aside from adorning themselves with a few modest innovative projects to give the appearance of being progressive. With the country experiencing such social disarray, we were convinced that at last the motivation to make changes would be high.

University and college campuses across North America were in crisis, many to the point of being almost ungovernable. Protests against the Vietnam War and nuclear arms threatened political stability. The social, health and educational organizations we were investigating in our study seemed overwhelmed by the radical cultural and behavioural upheaval of the young people they were attempting to serve. The Project 70 Study, as it came to be known, concluded, to no one's surprise, that the current needs of youth required institutions and organizations serving this population to engage in a major transformation. As one young person interviewed in the study put it so succinctly, the purpose of the agency, which was providing him with mental-health care was "to mind fuck me back into the Dark Ages." Under such incredibly irreverent and disruptive circumstances, many youth-serving organizations could not help but flounder. It seemed the right time to make major changes before the professional and bureaucratic establishment began to close ranks.

As noted earlier, Project 69 and Project 70 attempted to provide some hint as to the new and more collaborative approaches social agencies could use in working with youth. In 1970 the agencies had an opportunity to test out their effectiveness under serious crisis conditions. This year marked the terrible Kent State massacre, a situation where the National Guard of Ohio turned its weapons against university students demonstrating against the Vietnam War. Outrage among young people coalesced immediately across North America. More militant subgroups even went so far as to use the incident as a call to arms. In Toronto a major demonstration against the U.S. consulate on University Avenue was called and word had it that there would be thousands of young people attending and some would be armed. Project 70 met in emergency session to plan out a strategy to defuse the violent potential of the demonstration. I recall a worker from the Queen Street Mental Health Centre suggesting to Jack Ackroyd, who would later become Toronto's chief of police, that he should get an elephant from the Toronto Zoo and ride down University Avenue on its back posing as Elmer the Safety Elephant's trainer. Given the extensive use of street theatre at the time, this ridiculous idea possessed a certain charm. There was also no doubt among us that a little humour might well defuse the potential for the demonstration to turn into a riot.

In the end, however, we settled for a less dramatic intervention. We would have youth workers and volunteers infiltrate the demonstration and when anyone saw the slightest evidence of violence brewing they would move in and admonish the individual with a simple comment, consistent with the non-violent flower-power ethic of the day. "Hey man, are you crazy or something? Put that rock down," or "Put that weapon away." The strategy proved successful during the actual demonstration and it was only later, when the formal demonstration was over, that a number of hotheads went into the city's business section and committed some property damage.

Of course, it was only a collaborative response to a serious crisis but it showed what could be done if all the youth-serving organizations in the city got together to solve problems. Less dramatic parallel collaborations occurred many times during the years of Project 70 and its later incarnation, the Toronto Youth Services Network. In the end, however, only a few of the oddballs around the table established themselves as social service leaders. Gradually the system and a new era of growing professionalism and bureaucratic controls absorbed their creative vision, allowing only flashes of innovation to prevail. I was to learn an important lesson at this point, which was to haunt me throughout the remainder of my career. Unless threatened with extinction, public institutions and systems are incapable of making major changes either to their priorities or the way they do their work. Modest incremental change is the best you can hope to achieve even under the most pressing external conditions. The premier and the minister of health made some encouraging remarks about our study, the media covered the story for a week, a few indignant agency directors wrote letters to the editor and the report was shelved in the archives of Queen's Park. It was a response I was to experience many times over when invited to undertake studies for government.

The appearance of concern and change is what is important in the political world. Thus, it's not so important to actually resolve a social problem. The principal political agenda is to be seen to resolve the problems of people in need at minimum expenditure. I was to see this approach used time and again throughout my career, and it's just as immoral today as when it was first introduced in the 1960s and 1970s. It would be interesting to see how many public dollars are spent on smoke and mirrors, but that's a topic beyond my reach in this book.

Unlike the private sector, where market demands draw a quick response from corporations, public institutions are buffered against change by the flow of government and charitable dollars and by a complex array of professional, union and management relationships. Thus, the status quo is a comfortable mode of operation, particularly for organizations that have grown large and lazy. Creative innovation in the delivery of social programs seems to be the preserve of younger and smaller organizations or is relegated to the margins of large agency operations.

In the small town of Atlin in northern British Columbia it is said that if you don't like the weather, wait awhile and it's sure to change. Governments and institutions respond in similar fashion to troubling conditions. The social and cultural revolutionary wave, precipitated by the youth counterculture during the late 1960s and early 1970s, dissipated into a number of slow, meandering streams of change by the mid-1970s. The fashions, music and language of the period were gradually absorbed by mainstream commercial interests who recognized the potential for profit. The Vietnam War, a rallying point for so much of the rebellion, came to an end. The spiritual and political idealism of the founders of the counterculture revolution seemed lost on the next generation of young people. Finally the 1960s young people grew up and began worrying about jobs, mortgages and starting families. A few diehards ended up in communes and in remote communities such as Atlin, where many still march to the tune of a different drummer. By and large they are delightful people.

Although we didn't appreciate it at the time, the 1960s counterculture revolution was a phenomenon born of prosperity. For the most part, hippies were the sons and daughters of the suburban middle class. Very few of the young people wandering Yorkville, Haight-Ashbury or Long Beach on Vancouver Island came from poor or working-class families. In fact, I noted with interest that drug consumption in the downtown Toronto schools bordering the Yorkville area was considerably lower than that found in schools in Etobicoke, as well as in other middle-income Toronto suburbs. I concluded from this that when something is common in your culture, you can't express rebellion. Thus, suburban kids were rebelling against their parents' middle-class values, while inner-city kids were furthering their studies in an effort to get to college or university. Furthering your education was certainly an act opposite to the norms found in inner-city neighbourhoods, as I had discovered personally.

Likewise, on university campuses, which were prime sites of political upheaval, the most radical student leaders were most often the children of well-educated, middle-class parents. Dr. Taylor Statten, Jr., at the University of Toronto's Health Services noted in a survey he conducted at the time that the most militant of these radicals came almost exclusively from prosperous families where the parents held a decidedly liberal perspective. As it turned out, there was considerable angst in being comfortable and middle class in the late 1960s.

While society and its institutions were certainly shaken by the seismic scale of the 1960s cultural revolution, after teetering for five years or so they settled back onto their foundations. On the surface there was little evident physical damage to Canada's agencies and institutions. However, the meandering streams of new ideas and changed attitudes had soaked deeply into the society. The cautious, frugal and respectful behaviour that had been the standard for my formative years was swept away by a new generation of young people who would be caught between challenging tradition and seeking their own comfort and pleasure. These baby boomers, as they came to be called, would come to dominate Canada's social, economic and political life well into the early years of the new millennium. Unlike their parents, they would not satisfy themselves with the hope of eventual security and pleasure, or live through the promise of their children's lives. Through the ever-increasing prosperity that surrounded them, baby boomers would unfetter their lives from the social traditions and restraints of the past and live freely and generously for today. This dramatic change in the dominant public attitude would eventually challenge the social principles upon which Canada's version of the welfare state was founded. Sadly for me, my wife and I balanced successful careers while ignoring the essential elements of both our personal development and our relationship, resulting in an inevitable split. The social upheaval surrounding us was now being felt as personal upheaval.

The transformation of Canadian society from a culture of collective concern for the well-being of all citizens to one in which the rights of the individual citizen are paramount was ironically obscured by the symptoms of that transformation. The social upheavals of the late 1960s and 1970s, the rise of feminism, the rebellion of youth against the old social order and the emancipation of minority groups through new policies of multiculturalism were not only essential strands in the fabric of a "Just Society"; they heralded the new cultural era of self-absorption and individualism. The freeing of the marketplace paralleled the freeing of the individual from the constraints of the old societal order. Increasingly, cultural values were shifting. Individuals were being asked to "be their own best friend" and "look out for number one." While this was a very liberating experience for women, youth and certain social classes and cultural groups, it significantly reduced the critical role of personal relationships. The historic bond of looking after one another was to be discarded, as self-dedication became the dominant guiding principle for human behaviour.

This shift from personally looking after your family, friends and neighbours, to expecting individuals and families to look after themselves presented the ideal condition for the blossoming of the welfare state and the programs of social agencies. "Let government and professionals assume social responsibility so that I can be unfettered from my personal obligations to my extended family and neighbours." Adam Smith never foresaw the day when his free-market economic principles would be transferred to human relationships and civic life.

In April 1974 I accepted the position of executive director of the Family Service Association of Metro Toronto, one of Canada's oldest and most distinguished social agencies. In fact, it was FSA that helped to establish the country's first social-work training program at the University of Toronto in the early 1920s.

Indicative of the resistance to the change dynamic that occupies so much of the time and energy of the professions and social agencies, my appointment as the agency's first non–social work executive director was met with immediate disapproval by the Ontario Association of Professional Social Workers. For several weeks a flurry of angry letters littered the "Letters to the Editor" column of *The Globe and Mail*, and my social-work staff at the agency received letters from OAPSW'S president promising official support if it chose to resist my appointment. It took some 10 years to restore the relationship, but this was done by a new OAPSW executive in 1984 with the awarding of an Honorary Life Membership.

Meanwhile, the attention of my friends and colleagues in social services was sharply focused upon the specific episodes of the social upheaval. As a result, we were oblivious at the time to the deep cultural implications of the major social upheaval that swelled around us. As the new executive director of Metro Toronto's Family Service Association, I found myself thrust into the cauldron of this social transformation. At the time I recognized a few of the symptoms. Many individuals who for too long had lost any sense of self due to an overwhelming load of personal obligations were rightly joyous over the discovery of their personal freedom. The helping professions and social agencies busied themselves consolidating their sudden gains and growing sense of professionalism. And the general public celebrated the rapid advance in pensions, health care, unemployment insurance, welfare and greatly improved services.

The fact that the frail elderly, the disabled, the poor and children with special needs were now being more adequately supported by the state and social agencies was also a major liberating force for many Canadian families and individuals, particularly women. While I can look fondly at my parents' and grandparents' generations, when families and neighbours took sole responsibility for looking after the elderly and those family members with special needs, the quality and adequacy of care often left a great deal to be desired.

Throughout my reflections on the transition period between personal duties and obligations and collective entitlements and universality, I am struck by my own ambivalence, even to this day. I'm not one, as I've now said several times, who can look back with fondness to some fanciful Norman Rockwell golden era. I've been there and it wasn't like that, except for the privileged few. I do, however, cherish the values passed on to me by my parents. Likewise, I look at the era of rights and entitlements and recognize that the intent was noble to some degree. The problem, however, was that professional self-interest and human greed usurped the underlying purpose for universal entitlements. None of us, myself included, pointed to the corruption this wrought to the founding premise of the social-welfare state, namely adequate and prompt help for those suffering any form of deprivation under exceptional circumstances.

At some level I did recognize that the transition would require a balance between state, personal and civic involvement in the realignment of social responsibility and obligations. Perhaps that's why I fought so hard against the growing professional rigidity of social agencies, service systems and the bureaucratic bastions of government ministries. Likewise, I was more than a little concerned with the abandonment of individual and collective social responsibility. While there was clearly a need to correct serious imbalances in social responsibilities and obligations among significant sectors in society, the largest being women, the personal expression of rights and freedoms must not detract from each individual's fundamental responsibility in caring for his or her family, friends and community. The state was in no position to assume primary social responsibility for family and friends.

Under normal circumstances, when things are not going according to plan, you acknowledge the problem, correct it and move on. Alas, governments don't like making mistakes. Their political advisors tell them it costs votes. Just look at the defensive attitude that occurs in all legislatures when government has blundered. My God, a premier's or prime minister's popularity ratings could go down, a minister could get sacked or seats could be lost in by-elections. Thus, the political system has developed a protective immune system, which makes it terribly allergic to error. This is probably why so much money is spent on spin- doctors.

Of course, the very real danger existed in my new senior role with FSA that I could be gradually seduced by my rapid ascent to power. In 1974 I was only 37 years of age and now a central player within the "system." In the opinion of my old friend George Richards, I had sold out to the establishment. Increasingly, discussions between George and me turned to arguments as to whether anyone can ever successfully change a system from within. I pointed out to George that he could continue the good fight from outside the system because he had a paycheque coming from Crown Life Insurance, where he now worked as a senior systems analyst with the new computer technology that was just being introduced to business. George countered by pointing out that I had become yet another bureaucrat, at least three steps removed from our YMCA street work days with troubled kids.

He was without family and had fierce intellectual hostility toward traditional institutions, and his anger would eventually cause him to destroy himself. Though 25 years too late to be called a beatnik, George maintained the role of angry young man with incredible conviction and fortitude. As my intellectual superior and close personal friend throughout those transitional years when we both struggled to extricate ourselves from our working-class roots, I found the growing conflict between us both painful and confusing. George had planted enough doubt in my mind as to the real prospects of changing institutions or systems from within that I continued to query my real motivation long after our friendship collapsed.

Several years later I sat around a campfire with friends talking about my recent appointment as the president of the Donner Canadian Foundation. Colin Hamilton, a good friend and fellow executive director, looked at me quizzically and said, if I can translate it from the Long Branch vernacular, "You know, Couchman, this job could turn you into a real jerk." Colin was a Lakeshore boy who came from the same working-class roots as I did. After this remark and a good chuckle, I suddenly thought of the admonishment of my friend George Richards.

Having made the deliberate choice to attempt change from within the system, I turned my vocational energies toward making it happen. Nevertheless, the seduction of personal security, success and stability remained very real influences. I had to fight consciously not to allow them to ease me into the comfortable status quo. In this struggle I developed an acute personal sense of why our social-welfare system was evolving in directions that could not have been predicted or foreseen by my parents' generation and the architects of the social-welfare state. Hardship was constantly in their face and the idea that someday you could have it all, without sacrifice and pain, was beyond their imagination. In the end, however, they had a better grip on reality than did their children and grandchildren. We were eased into the myth of social comfort by an unprecedented period of sustained economic growth.

I had discovered, as most adults do, that life is not simple nor is it static. It can also be desperately lonely, if one is not grounded by a loving and secure family and close friends. My personal awareness of these basic human needs made the fight against human alienation and the personal isolation of poverty that much more vigorous. I was also fired up in my aspirations by the growing doubt that institutional and systemic resistance to change might make serious incremental change impossible, unless people could overcome this resistance.

Certainly, in the early 1970s all the external indicators for positive change looked promising, particularly given the heavyweight intellectual leadership now at the helm of Canada's federal government. We lived in prosperous times and, even with the OPEC oil crisis of the early 1970s, no one doubted for a minute that economic growth would continue, even if it required operating for a brief period in a deficit position. This illusion would, of course, be fuelled by the optimism and appetites of the baby-boom generation, whose members were gradually making their way into the junior levels of the professions and government bureaucracies which controlled Canada's social programs. The shift in social values and attitudes, precipitated by the demographic dominance of Canada's young adult population and continuing economic growth, was slowly but effectively jostling the frugal values and cautions of the older generation into the social and political background. Remember, this new generation of leaders grew out of the heady idealism of the late 1960s, and the era's passion for peace, love and social justice was the basis for their humane instincts. These instincts, in turn, led to actions and policies which seemed like the right thing to do. Having never experienced normal budgetary conditions, they were under the illusion that they could have it all. Social justice could therefore be achieved without loss of comfort and security.

As you can see (as I have been able to do in retrospect), none of us were very conscious of the complex motivations and issues that had to be grasped in order to steer a reasoned course into the future. I firmly believed that I could, through my efforts to develop innovative programs, change the course of the social-service juggernaut. All I needed to do was be in a place of influence to encourage creative people to dream of what might be and then take the required risks to achieve those dreams.

What I didn't understand, however, was that an executive director is primarily an administrator whose job it is to manage human and financial resources, ensure good public relations, maintain a political balance between board members and staff and ensure sufficient income so the agency is able to do the job. Being a highly creative program innovator is not a requirement of the job; in fact, it generally places you in conflict with those tasks deemed essential in your job description. It was somewhat ironic that I had spent much of my career struggling to achieve sufficient power so as to implement good ideas. Now that I finally had the authority required to make changes, I found that I was forced to see my program vision become an addendum to my primary management obligations.

One other thing forcefully struck me about family-service work, as it did about all other forms of so-called human services. Agencies, institutions and organizations tend to confine themselves to their own systems. Thus, health care generally limits its co-operative involvement to hospitals, clinics, public health and doctors in private practice. Likewise, universities and colleges talk among themselves, as do school boards. The junior cousins of human services, namely social agencies, probably talk more about collaborating with organizations outside the social-service systems. However, they probably are as ineffective in their attempted collaborations as anyone else. Of course, the systemic isolation of each sector is reinforced by the rigid structure of government, which sets distinct policies and regulations for each system, in fact, for discrete sets of organizations within a specific system. Government maintains this segregation by funding each system separately.

I recall feeling enormously frustrated with the silo structure of the human-service systems when I learned one day in the late 1970s that the social-work services of the Toronto Board of Education were to practise a more limited response to student problems. Instead of offering counselling to children and their families, they were now directed to simply identify problem students and refer them to a family-service agency or children's mental-health clinic for even limited counselling. This direction from the board was a response to reduced grants caused by declining school enrollments. The demographic wave of baby boomers had now moved on from the school system into colleges, universities and employment. As a result, cutbacks were required. This, of course, is where professional power politics came into play. The first sacrificial lambs were counselling services, special education and library resources. While eventually there would have to be reductions in teaching staff, the power of teachers' federations staved this off until the bitter end. In the meantime, support services were decimated.

In any event, when the board of education decided to limit the role of school social workers, I took a quick tally of our resources by adding up all the family counsellors working in Toronto's four family-services agencies. The most generous estimate showed that we had one counsellor for every 22,500 residents of Metro Toronto. Our mental-health resources had the same limitations. Eighteen percent of all young people in the city were assessed as having serious emotional or mental disabilities. This suggested a potential population of 137,500 troubled young people residing in Metro at the time. Any serious thought that social and mental-health services could meet the needs of this group of young people was ridiculous. But, of course, there were no mechanisms for various partners coming together to analyze and plan solutions to the problem. The fact that the school board decided to refer all its troubled students to an already overburdened family-service and children's mental-health system, without consulting anyone but themselves, was evidence of the silo mentality of the system.

What was more troublesome, however, was the failure of Ontario's ministry bastions and the metro organizations funded by these respective ministries to assume any responsibility for collectively addressing the service needs of their troubled children and their families. Toronto and Ontario were no better or no worse than other cities or provinces in Canada at co-ordinating resources in an effective manner. Nor was the issue an insoluble dilemma. It was simply a low priority and, silly though the actions of local school boards and other social and health agencies might be, the will was lacking to correct the problem. And, quite frankly, I was deeply concerned that, even if the will should suddenly coalesce to take collective action, institutions and professions would pursue their own agendas on how best to deal with troubled children and their families. Autonomy and system stability had superseded the best interests of children and does to this day.

To be effective, product and service demand must be driven by consumer need and interest. What had occurred as a result of silo thinking by professions and governments was a belief that professionals and bureaucrats know what is best for people. The Canadian welfare state, however, was founded as a result of people identifying their needs. Governments resisted these demands for some time, but in the end were driven by public demand. We now live in a situation where people don't know what is good for them. Or this is what the professions and bureaucrats believe.

Having institutions and professionals assume total responsibility is not the way families and communities solve their problems. Generally speaking, you rely on family, friends and neighbours as being the first line of defence in looking after people's social needs. Educating the young and attending to basic health care are also largely done informally by one's family and friends. You only call upon doctors, social workers, nurses, psychologists and other helping professionals when a problem becomes very severe or you don't enjoy a close network of family and friends to help out during normal periods of need and distress. It is also evident that volunteers, teachers, recreation specialists and clergy often serve as principal helpers with quite troubled or needy individuals within a community, apart from the work done by professionals specifically trained to deal with such problems.

While this reality seems self-evident, it was certainly not well understood by the majority of professionals or senior government bureaucrats in the 1970s and early 1980s. Their attention was fully occupied in creating the new social vision for Canada's welfare state. In this process they were busy consolidating their power bases within the bureaucracies of governments and organizations. They therefore saw little purpose in supporting natural approaches to personal care. Building phalanxes of professional caregivers was the order of the day within their burgeoning empires.

Fortunately FSA was free from the directions and regulations of government, unlike our colleagues in the child welfare sector whose directions were being set by government. Given the fact we received much of our financial support from the United Way and through fees for our services, we could afford to be more creative and entrepreneurial in the design and delivery of our services. In this regard, FSA came as close to being a market-driven organization as any social agency. Without major government support we were dependent on our clients and our program creativity to maintain growth. Any rationalization that we could build an effective system of family-service care with such limited resources was just plain blind and stupid.

As an example of the entrepreneurial spirit in 1976, under the leadership of Brock Colby, FSA's service director for the agency's eastern region, and with the help of Audrey McLaughlin at the Canadian Mental Health Association, we launched the first comprehensive employee-assistance program in Canada at the Warner Lambert Company. Audrey McLaughlin went on, of course, to attempt to change the system from within and largely met the same success as I myself did.

During the next decade, however, FSA's family-counselling program was extended to 20 companies, thereby generating over $1 million in new revenue for the agency.

In addition, we enlisted Family Service Canada in developing a national employee-assistance program for family-service agencies across the country, thereby making the entire system a major provider of both not-for-profit as well as profit-making counselling. Introduced during the peak years of fully subsidized government social programs, the Family Service Association of Metro Toronto's employee-assistance program was to become a model for other non-profit/corporate collaborative service efforts in the 1990s.

It was clearly beyond the reasonable capacity of the social-service system to provide a complete range of social programs on a universal basis, despite the intention of some policy architects. As noted previously, the original intention of the founders of the welfare state was to provide essential help during periods of personal crisis, as well as offering ongoing support to those few disabled individuals unable to provide for themselves. By the mid-1970s these limited objectives had suffered a mortal wound, the principle of universality.

It was reasoned by policy experts and some politicians that social programs could be smoothly marketed if they were readily available to all citizens. Many politicians also recognized that by pandering to the desires of middle-class voters more votes could be won. Thus, certain social programs became viewed as a right, rather than a resource to be used during exceptional circumstances. With social responsibility being shifted from personal care to care by the state and professionally run agencies, each of the government service silos produced its own sets of policies and regulations to ensure rigorous service and financial accountability. Slowly, incentives for creative new program initiatives were thwarted by the risk-averse leadership of the various government bureaucracies. While there were individual instances of bureaucrats attempting to encourage service innovation in communities, the culture quickly moved to one of conservative caution and control. Resistance to change was thus solidly integrated into the top-down service systems of the Canadian welfare state.

By the late 1970s "the bloom was off the rose" so to speak. Mounting deficits began to slow service expansion in the social services. What little creativity still existed in the system was subtly discouraged as the requirement to cut rather than to build services became the order of the day. To this day, rather than address fundamental reform, it is easier for government to axe whole programs and downsize services than to unleash what creative potential may remain in agencies and the social-service system. Government does this in a totally irrational manner, oblivious to the human consequences of its actions.

Chapter 5

Politics
and
Resistance to Change

In the early 1980s I renewed a conversation I had had with Jack Ackroyd, chief of police for Metro Toronto, about strengthening our combined services to women victims of domestic violence. According to police statistics, most incidents of domestic violence tend to occur between 8:00 p.m. and midnight, with some of the most severe cases occurring in the early hours of the morning. Violence rates rise significantly on Friday, Saturday and Sunday evenings as compared to weeknights. Jack had been quick to point out to me that the reason police were referring so few cases of domestic violence to the family-service agencies was that the agencies were never open when the majority of domestic problems occurred. Also, he noted that when referrals were attempted, the waiting lists prevented the required quick response that serious domestic violence situations demand.

When I first became aware of the dilemma in the mid-1970s I talked with Jack, who was then deputy chief of police, about the possibility of pairing police officers with social workers to deal directly and quickly with incidents of domestic violence when they first erupt. This

Domestic Response Team, as it came to be later called, could deal with the extreme difficulties of the initial incident and ensure that referrals for follow-up were promptly and smoothly addressed. Jack liked the idea but indicated that the time was not right to introduce such a radical new concept to policing services. As he put it, it would require a Herculean effort to change attitudes and behaviour within the police culture to accommodate the idea of police officers and social workers working as a team in frontline police work. Such a change would demand ongoing support from the highest level of the department as well as extensive training.

When Jack Ackroyd became chief of police in the early 1980s, the time was right to reintroduce the idea of establishing the Domestic Response Team. True to his convictions and his word, Chief of Police Ackroyd acted promptly and the Domestic Response Team, or DRT as it came to be known, was established as a pilot project in 13 Division, which encompassed much of the City of York in Metro Toronto.

While there were some initial struggles adjusting to one another's cultures, police officers from the Community Officers Division and FSA social workers soon melded into effective teams. We chose a male/female mix for each team, and as the DRT was in plain clothes, it was often difficult for the public to discern who was the police officer and who was the social worker. This was often the case when the officer was a woman and the social worker a male.

Following the early success of the DRT pilot project, the model was quickly expanded to encompass several more divisions. What was more impressive about the project were the secondary benefits that gradually began to occur as a result of the collaboration. The police began to appreciate that domestic violence was not a private family matter that simply required the occasional appearance of an authority figure to restore the peace. Not only were the police persuaded to treat domestic assaults as violent crimes, but the officers also began to receive training from members of DRT during their college preparation and in-service training programs in how to manage such situations. Likewise, social workers and family counsellors became more tuned to the nature of family violence and recognized that such situations demand high-priority handling and a special set of skills.

As the program's early success became known and the public profile of the project grew, so also did professional resistance. It became clear that such collaborations across systems had implications. Program priorities would be forced to shift, more sensitive approaches to the management of human crisis would have to be found and, most important of all, the professions might have to give up some of their hard-fought jurisdictional ground. When Jack Ackroyd retired as chief, the forces of resistance would rebound and soon dismantle the Domestic Response Team. Like so many such systemic battles, the politics would become incredibly complex and time consuming. With Jack Marks, the new chief of police, being extremely sensitive to building an internal support base for his leadership, it soon became clear that he would side with the more vociferous reactionary elements within the police force. Once senior leadership support was lost, the DRT was doomed. Under the guise of attempting to reduce expenditures, the most common rationalization used by agencies and institutions to rid themselves of troublesome innovation, DRT responsibility was transferred to the Salvation Army's victim assistance services. Within a year, any progressive remnant of the DRT was lost.

It was with some irony that six months after the demise of the DRT I read a newspaper clipping about our Domestic Response Team, published by the *Manchester Guardian*. The article was sent to me by my daughter, Barbara, who was living in the U.K. The article spoke about the difficulties that British police were having in dealing effectively with domestic violence. The columnist went on to praise the work of the Toronto Police Department, which had created something called "Domestic Response Teams." He suggested that this fine approach might be tried in Britain. I was tempted to send the article to Chief Marks but resisted, as it would have only further entrenched the defensiveness of the Toronto Police Department. As far as I know the British police were also able to resist this innovation.

Yet another initiative that confirmed the need for interagency alliances occurred in the late 1970s when a dynamic young social worker was introduced to me by a colleague. Bruno Scorsone — an Italian raised in Argentina and educated in the U.S. and Canada — expressed concern that Italian and Portuguese immigrant families with mentally challenged children were not receiving adequate attention and care. From all that he said it appeared that these ethnic families were being bypassed by the agencies established to care for their needs. Part of the reason given was that the agencies didn't have the language capacity or cultural knowledge to serve Toronto's increasingly diverse ethnic communities.

Scorsone's assignment was to reach out to Toronto's large Italian and Portugese communities to see how families with mentally retarded (now called mentally challenged) children could be helped. In short order, he assisted with the establishment of several self-help groups, with a total membership of over 200 parents. Scorsone turned to an unlikely source of help to achieve this, namely the Catholic churches serving these two populations. No one had thought to involve this natural source of aid as the church was outside the social-service system. Though once a critical part of the system right up to the end of the Great Depression, its role had been gradually usurped by professionally led agencies.

I likened the experience to building bridges between sectors and organizations that are in the same business but are under different professional or government auspices. Alas, as with the Domestic Response Team, resistance was close to insurmountable. One gets bone weary dealing with the subtle politics in establishing such ventures. When you gain positive profile, the adversary goes back into the woods. However, as soon as an opportunity arises the opposition launches a series of rockets known as constructive criticisms. These are consciously or unconsciously designed to weaken the effort. Only the most valiant walk to the outhouse as a tornado sweeps toward them. It's safer to hunker down in the root cellar. I won't pursue this metaphor out of respect to my editor's sensitivities, but I leave it to the reader's imagination as to how one relieves oneself under such conditions.

In my estimation, the Hon. Marc Lalonde was one of the few federal ministers with the courage and intelligence to attempt the task of altering the course of Canada's welfare-state programs. Had he been successful in his efforts, we might well have averted the dismemberment of Canada's national social programs. However, for many of the same reasons cited above, resistance was overwhelming.

By the mid-1970s it had become evident to more knowledgeable observers of Canada's social programs that public expectations were creating a fiscal and administrative morass of programs under the Canada Assistance Plan, introduced in 1966 as a policy framework for Canada's social programs. With expenditures rising and the complexity of various social-transfer programs increasing, Lalonde recognized the need to consolidate the patchwork quilt of unemployment, disability and welfare programs that had developed over the years. In the mid-1970s Marc Lalonde, as minister of health and welfare, took the bold step of proposing the Guaranteed Annual Income. The concept behind the GAI was to consolidate most of Canada's welfare and benefit programs so that no Canadian would ever again live in extreme poverty.

Utilizing the tax system to determine income and distribute benefits would also have eliminated several layers of bureaucracy that were then in place to administer the myriad of federal and provincial benefit programs. It was a superb rationalization of welfare-state policy, designed to get the necessary job done as efficiently as possible. It was apparent to Lalonde and to many of us in the mid-1970s that Canada's system of social-transfer programs could not continue to evolve in such a fractured and poorly co-ordinated manner. While it was by no means a perfect concept, Lalonde published an orange paper on the Guaranteed Annual Income proposal and requested Canadians to respond with helpful design improvements and suggestions.

The Guaranteed Annual Income was attacked immediately by both the right and the left of Canada's political spectrum. To conservatives it was seen as a disincentive to work. It was simply too easy to access. To the left, which included the Canadian labour movement, the GAI had the potential to discourage low-end salary growth, as employers might come to rely upon the Guaranteed Annual Income to top up low wages. Those of us who appreciated that the welfare state must evolve if it was going to sustain itself failed miserably in providing the essential support Lalonde required for gaining Cabinet approval of his proposal. When I spoke with him in Calgary at a meeting of the Canadian Council on Social Development, he indicated that only five significant Canadian organizations had responded to his request for suggestions. One of these organizations was, thankfully, the Social Action Committee of the Family Service Association of Metro Toronto.

Marc Lalonde later confided to me that the concept for the GAI was ultimately killed at a Cabinet meeting when John Turner, then minister of finance, produced a highly negative letter from a professional antipoverty activist living in the Regent Park Housing Development. With support for the GAI hanging in the balance, Turner read the letter aloud and concluded, "You see, Marc, not even the poor support the idea." I knew the activist quite well and explained to Lalonde, all too late, that his work was funded by a grant from labour.

Resistance to change comes in many guises. It can also be effectively cloaked, as it was in the 1970s and 1980s, by both right- and left-wing political polarities. As the executive director of the Family Service Association, and as a board member of the Metro Social Planning Council and chair of the Etobicoke Social Planning Council, I came to appreciate that the vested interests of business and labour must be taken into account when attempting to promote progressive social-policy reform.

In my estimation, the defeat of the proposed Guaranteed Annual Income was a defining moment in the development of Canada's social programs. Up to this stage we had managed to effectively appeal to the hearts and common sense of Canadians in reducing human misery. The attainment of social justice and the well-being of all Canadians was the dominant collective dynamic in working toward a new social contract. The values and attitudes of my parents' and grandparents' generations had prevailed in creating social stability and personal security for all Canadians. Suddenly, self-interest emerged as a pivotal force in shaping Canada's social programs. The critical balance between collective social responsibility and the frugal management of precious resources was lost in the struggle over the GAI. Donald McDonald would try once more in his 1982 Royal Commission on the Economic Union and Development Prospects for Canada to introduce the idea of a GAI. Despite the promise that such an approach held for real reform, it was simply too great a threat for too many special-interest groups. Not until Lloyd Axworthy, the minister of human resources, made his faltering attempt to fundamentally reform Canada's welfare-state programs in 1993–1994 would a federal minister have the courage to even consider such an important project. Axworthy, like Lalonde, would fail in his attempts due to the influence of another powerful minister of finance, in this instance Paul Martin, Jr. In both situations the political reputations of the two ministers were damaged by their thwarted efforts to engage in major reform of Canadian social programs. Even when the facts are on the table, real social reform is a terribly unpopular political cause. No one but no one at the federal level tampers with Canada's "sacred trust" and comes out unscathed, as Prime Minister Mulroney was to discover.

It would take 20 years following the efforts of Marc Lalonde to con-structively overhaul Canada's welfare-state programs, to muster suffi-cient public support to address essential social-policy reform. When it did occur, many of the programs were so tired, expensive and ineffective that the federal government had little trouble sweeping them under the carpet of the provincial governments, using the guise that the imple-mentation of social policy had always been a provincial jurisdictional issue anyway.

By the early 1980s the booming prosperity of the post-war years was clearly over. Families could no longer sustain the income growth they had taken for granted for so many years, and with their material appetites having been so well conditioned for so many years, more and more women found themselves in the workforce simply to preserve the living standards of their families.

The recession of 1981–1982 came as a particularly strong shock to personal security. The jobless recovery, a new phenomenon, heralded the onset of a major economic transition. Like other countries in the Western world, Canada was moving from the modern industrial era to an era of technological change. Information and communication tech-nology had precipitated the change, but the forces of global economics and free trade propelled it at a rate unforeseen in the lifetimes of any of us. Given the incredible force of these changes to people's working lives, and the stress it imposed on family life, the tattered remnants of Canada's social safety net, which was designed during an unprece-dented era of industrial growth, now found itself overwhelmed by human insecurity this new economic era. The collapse of the Canadian welfare state was thus inevitable, as it was in almost all countries of the Western world.

And so there we had it: public greed, unassailable bastions of pro-fessionals and bureaucratic power and mounting public debt. Resistance to change had been refined to a highly skilled art form and there was a total lack of political will and leadership courage: the course was set to allow the welfare state to implode upon itself. Having effec-tively transferred social responsibility to the state, Canadians were now incapable of reasserting their individual and collective concern for the well-being of friends and neighbours in need.

By this point in my career I was no longer seen as the feisty young youth worker and teacher whose little experimental pilot projects could be tolerated. I had become very much part of the social-welfare establishment. I did, of course, continue in my efforts to shake the system by doing things differently. However, I realized one day that I was tired and had lost my creative edge. Thankfully, however, I still was capable of recognizing other people's creative ideas.

One day Mary Clark, one of our social workers involved with spousal abuse, came to me with a remarkable piece of lateral thinking. Her husband, David, a corporate leader, had just returned from an Outward Bound course and, hearing about the abused women, realized the course's potential benefits for these women. Here I was the chair of Outward Bound and the executive director of the Family Service Association and I'd missed this possible connection. I confess it had never dawned on me that there could be such a beneficial connection, even though I have constantly advocated alliances between institutions and across professions. And so Outward Bound's Women of Courage Program was born. I smacked myself on the head and vowed to remain alert.

I had fought so hard to make major changes to the traditional social-service system, with negligible results. It slowly dawned on me that far more significant changes might be effected by exploring simpler alternative initiatives that crossed over between formal counselling and social case-work services and the types of recreation experiences I had personally been falling back on during periods of confusion and stress. Up to now progress in social services seemed to be correlated with increasing the range of professional intervention in people's lives and spending more money on new transfer-payment programs.

Though the system was now no longer operative, there was still the challenge of seeing whether crisis might be just the incentive required to jolt my little piece of the system back on track, sort of a heart-defibrillator effect. Clearly government, closed professional systems and traditional organizations had become anathemas to change. But could something be reawakened in the collective public consciousness that would cause people to say enough is enough, folks? Certainly more and more children were living in poverty; there were now homeless people visible on the streets; people could no longer be assured of getting thorough medical attention and care; and ridiculous things kept happening to people whose special needs were all too obvious. Would a healthy dose of public anxiety begin to seep through the cracks of our creaky social-service system?

I realized, of course, that there were some fundamental questions that had to be considered if real change were to occur. Some of these had to deal with the mechanics of the system, the silo effect, distorted accountability and something far more elusive — Canadian character.

It seemed to me that the feeling of entitlement, which had led to the program principle of universality, was encouraging many people and many corporations to seek money they didn't really need. This behaviour, in turn, was producing significant public deficits, and the country's debt was increasing to the point where over one-third of our tax revenues were going to debt-servicing charges. My parents certainly understood the need for spending deficits when Canada was at war. However, when the war was over they insisted upon their country paying off its debts. This was an attitude bred into them by a decade and a half of personal deprivation. Had some not-so-clever marketer introduced credit cards in the 1930s or 1940s, the idea would have fallen flat on its face. You saved, then paid for all goods and services in cash, with the exception of your house and perhaps your car.

Thus, character influences public policy and public policy affects character. The two forces feed off one another, as we will see. However, it's character that leads in this economic dance.

Once I left FSA in 1989 these issues and questions constantly occupied my thoughts as I pursued my career as president of the Donner Canadian Foundation, later as an independent consultant and, finally, as the executive director of the Yukon Family Services Association.

Chapter 6

Professionalism
and
Other Silos

The probing questions of professional isolation, accountability and character were causing me to have too many sleepless nights. And focusing on what questions to ask was not a sudden and clear process by any means. It was more a gradual process. Ever so slowly I became conscious that something was wrong with the way things were going. Another thing I began to appreciate was that my probing was very much a personal exercise, a sort of reflection on my years in the trenches. Also, I realized that I was no saint or purist. I had been part of the system, and while my efforts to change things for the better were continuous throughout my career, I too was seduced by the comforts of stability and security that I found within the system. However, I had also lived with increasing moral conflict. Not only was I haunted by my friend George Richards's admonishment about having sold out, I kept remembering my grandmother's and mother's experiences during the hardship they had faced. My mother, by the way, is still alive at 89 years of age and doesn't let me forget my roots.

Even my older son Stephen challenged my assumptions. In one instance during his university years he decided that it was not good enough to write about poverty in his sociology course; to understand it he had to live in its midst, even if only for a short while. One day he took off to live as a homeless person with only three quarters and a single subway token. The quarters were to be used to call me each day, and the subway token was to be used to get home. Over the next four days he slept on park benches, shared cheap sherry with some Aboriginal friends in a park, ate at soup kitchens and stared into the windows of restaurants and stores. From these experiences he wrote a play entitled *Glass Walls*, which he produced and acted in, in Peterborough where he attended Trent University.

The one thing that impressed him the most was his invisibility on the streets of downtown Toronto. Wherever he wandered there were glass walls. He would stare at people eating fine food in restaurants, only to have them avert their eyes. He would look at wonderful consumer goods in windows, but when he entered a store he would be quickly shown to an exit. His most memorable experience, however, was walking into St. James' Cathedral on Sunday morning, where his grandfather had been dean for many years. An usher politely asked him whether he didn't want to go to the parish hall for a bowl of soup. When he said no, he was shown promptly to the door. It, too, was made of glass.

His conclusion from this experience was that there are poor people and there are really poor people. The first category of people are the "deserving" poor. They receive modest government support. Really poor people, however, are considered undeserving, a category developed during the Middle Ages. These people are not welcome at the parish poor table but are quickly shown to the road leading out of town.

Your children are often your best teachers. Certainly Stephen's experience and his play *Glass Walls* both clarified some of the problems within our system and moved me deeply. I also, for the first time, recognized that not only do professionals operate within silos, but we also put people in need within silos.

Despite all my explanations and rationalizations, my Great Depression–era conscience was clearly getting the better of me. You can only twist your principles and values so far before something snaps. I knew that my need for recognition and financial security had made me part of the problem rather than the solution. I reasoned that my first love was program development. More and more, however, in my years as a senior manager, I was being expected to dig a bunker for the defence of my agency's services. The result was that I left the Family Service Association of Metro Toronto in 1989.

Leaving a position, however, does not resolve fundamental issues. Systemic change requires the patience of Job and a level of passionate fortitude known to few other than religious zealots. Clearly I had lost my patience and I had no aspirations to become a zealot. I also recognized that, unlike the zealot who seeks comfort in fundamentalism's assurances, I had many observations but few answers to the dilemma. I concluded, however, that the formula for effective change would have to encompass several key components within Canadian culture, well beyond the tinkering of social programs and services by social workers and other helping professionals. I concluded that the critical components are character and values, arrogant professional self-confidence and professional isolation, and the current system of public accountability.

While deliberation on such matters is largely the purview of academics, academia has proven itself to be part of the problem rather than a source for solutions. This is particularly true of university faculties such as education, social work and clinical psychology, as well as certain health disciplines. Besides, I had taught part time throughout the 1980s at the University of Toronto's Ontario Institute for Studies in Education and observed that once teachers, social workers or clinical psychologists remove themselves from frontline practice, they rapidly lose relevance as instructors in their respective disciplines. Their creative energies seem rapidly overwhelmed by the departmental and institutional politics that inevitably engulf the new instructor. Medicine is probably one of the few exceptions to this rule. While politics within departments of medicine are just as fierce as in other faculties, professors not only teach but they remain medical practitioners. My conclusion: we'd be unwise to look to universities or colleges for a thoughtful analysis of the problem, let alone possible solutions.

As for sociologists and political scientists, academics in two fields of study that might have something thoughtful to say about the situation, they appeared largely caught up in their own preservation. Besides, most of the disciplines speak their own particular language. This works well when they talk with one another, but it makes for difficulty when they try to talk with someone in another discipline. Having written articles for several academic journals, I know the flaw all too well. In fact, when I look back at some of my early work, I now have difficulty understanding what I was trying to say. And as for people working in the social-program field, they are largely seen by academics as aliens from another planet. I recall an instance, for example, when I was attempting to get applied-research funding to study the effects of divorce and separation on children caught in this family circumstance. Our proposal kept getting rejected by the federal social sciences group that hands out research dollars. It was only when enlightened by a helpful civil servant that I understood and was able to remedy the problem. Apparently, the members of the committee recommending approval of applied-research grants were all university academics. It would be unfair to say that they were simply trying to keep funding within the academic realm. Rather, I think that they simply were averse to having things placed before them in plain language. When I discovered this fact, I engaged an academic from the faculty of social work at the University of Toronto to translate our proposal into academic language. It was approved without difficulty and without substantive changes.

In another instance I recall being invited by the Canadian Association of Registered Psychologists to deliver a paper on social advocacy at its annual convention. More than 1,100 psychologists attended the meeting. As with most such professional gatherings, it was organized according the usual format: each day a keynote speaker followed simultaneous workshops in the morning and afternoons. Usually at lunch such gatherings have an inspirational speaker, someone who can talk in plain language and offer a compelling address containing humour and numerous anecdotes. The day I presented my paper there were eight workshops in my time slot. I drew seven people to my workshop and three were friends who had come along for moral support. Afterward we conferred on how such a topic could be so far off the mark. I had naturally assumed that psychologists were devoted to helping individuals and families restore themselves to healthy functioning and would be keen on looking at their discipline's role in addressing external issues that contribute to lack of good mental health (e.g., unemployment, poverty, job stress, lack of support for those with disabilities, inadequate child care, etc.). When I raised this point with the organizers, I was informed that these were issues that fell within the domain of social work, not psychology. Psychology is the scientific study of the human mind and its functions, particularly as they relate to behaviour. As one whose contextual roots are in philosophy, it was beyond my imagination that human behaviour can be isolated from culture and socioeconomic circumstance. This incident underscored my fear that we had created professional silos that had little relevance to helping people.

In like fashion, I saw that government human-service organization was structured along the same lines. Like the professions, government departments of health, education, justice, social services and recreation and culture had created comfortable silos for themselves, or as we say in the north, stovepipes. It is this silo structure of organization that encourages human-service disciplines to largely operate in isolation from one another. I asked myself, why had social programs evolved in this dysfunctional manner? After all, up to 200 years ago each of these areas of thought or practice was either housed in philosophy or theology. My simple conclusion was that the silo structure was a consequence of professional protectionism. It ultimately all had to do with autonomy and power.

Throughout much of my career I noted a related phenomenon, that of credentialing professionals. No one can teach, for example, who does not hold a teaching certificate. Likewise, you cannot call yourself a psychologist without having passed the rigorous standards of the Society of Registered Psychologists. And on we go with most of the other disciplines. In the north I've noted that wolves and bears stake out their territorial claims by urinating around the parameter of their claimed territories. Somehow I can't shake the image from my mind of social workers, psychologists, teachers and other human-care disciplines rushing around communities pissing out their claims for territorial turf.

It will be argued, of course, that the practice of these disciplines left a great deal to be desired when professionals were not credentialed. This is a valid concern. In the past harm was actually done to people because the so-called helper lacked adequate training and practice standards were non-existent. In one painful incident, I recall a social worker at FSA back in the 1970s asking a battered woman what she was doing to provoke the assaults against her. Such incidents occurred far too regularly and still do occur. The problem cannot be solved, however, simply by credentialing professionals.

At one point in the stampede to establish professional certification turf, the Ontario minister of health recognized the problem that this was creating for service integration. In 1974 Minister Tom Wells established a committee to study the matter and to come up with the basis for a mental-health disciplines act. Murray Ross, recently retired president of York University, was asked to serve as chair. He, in turn, invited me to join this committee as one of its six members. The first task we set ourselves was to identify all those disciplines that professed to be in the field of therapeutic mental health. In total we came up with 42 independent disciplines, everything from psychiatry, psychology and social work to pastoral counselling, addiction counselling, child-care work and bereavement therapy. While some were clearly lacking in basic scientific validity, the majority of the 42 disciplines had found an accepted role for themselves.

In the end the Mental Health Disciplines Committee, as our group was called, came up with seven practice categories. According to our ratings, all of the valid 42 disciplines could be categorized within one of the practice categories. At this point the Ministry of Health took our report out for consultation with the affected professional communities. As you can imagine, all hell broke loose as each discipline, except for those in the top category allowing independent practice, attempted to justify its claim to higher placement within the categories of practice. In the end the effort was doomed as there was no professional support for establishing a college of mental health disciplines. Public interest was thus overwhelmed by professional self-interest. To this day, any quack can still hang up a shingle saying that he or she is a "professional" counsellor.

Earlier in the book I make a strong plea for innovation. If our goal as a society is to improve the health and well-being of people, we can expect that there is a connection between the number of social workers, teachers, doctors, psychologists, etc. in specific communities, and the state of health and well-being of the community's residents. After all, our primary public expenditures in support of health and well-being are the number of services and programs offered to specific communities. As I consider the equation relating amount of dollars spent on services and programs and the actual health and well-being of people, I see little correlation. Of course, when essential services drop below a required level there is some correlation. Such is the case in Russia right now.

As evidence of the lack of correlation when adequate services and programs do exist, I have only to look at my community in the Yukon to see that the amount of service doesn't equate with the health and well-being of people. For example, the Yukon has the highest level of alcohol consumption per capita in Canada. Our women live nine fewer years than the average Canadian woman and our men seven years less than the average Canadian male. Furthermore, the Yukon has the highest rate of reformatory incarceration in the country, and rates of family violence and child abuse and neglect exceed all provincial norms.

When I considered the other side of the equation, namely the number of professionals engaged in treating these problems, I was astounded to find that the Yukon spends more per capita on professional services than practically any other jurisdiction in the country. For example, the ratio of family counsellors to population is one to 3,500. In Toronto the ratio at last count was one to 22,500.

It is not my intent to single out my community of the Yukon as an exceptional example of the lack of results for the amount of money spent. Similar situations can be found in many other regions of Canada. I must also point out with respect to the work of my Yukon colleagues that they work exceptionally hard and show remarkable compassion and sensitivity to the individuals and families whom they serve. However, when it comes to collaboration between health, justice, education and social services, the record in the Yukon is abysmal, as it is in most regions of the country. Those committed workers in communities who work in close co-operation and collaboration with one another do so in spite of the practice being informally discouraged by the ministry overseers. Of course, if one were to invite comment on this point from the officials, they would point to statements on the value of "harmonization" among their respective ministries. Scratch the veneer of this official rhetoric and you will quickly uncover armour-plated stovepipes that prevent serious collaboration. I hardly need to tell you that such a silo-structured culture is an anathema to innovation.

In one instance, for example, one of my counsellors at the Yukon Family Services Association encountered a teenaged boy with a serious psychiatric disorder. The syndrome from which he suffered made his functioning in the community and in school extremely problematic. At the community level the school personnel, social workers and health officials had exhausted their resources in attempting to support the lad and his family. As the boy's case was being monitored by the Children's Services Branch of the Ministry of Health and Social Services, I recommended that we hold a case conference to plan for the boy. Now, under any reasonable approach to this fairly standard procedure those departments involved with the child would be brought together. In this instance it would have involved school personnel and the school psychologist, probation authorities, child-welfare personnel, mental-health authorities, the police and my own agency. We were working with the family. On the day of the scheduled meeting I went over to the Children's Services Branch. Around the conference table sat seven officials. None, however, had been invited from health, education or from juvenile law enforcement. Every person was an official from the Children's Services Branch of Social Services. Furthermore, I was questioned as to why, as a minimally involved voluntary-sector organization, I had pushed to have such a conference convened. Needless to say, bureaucratic ranks closed around the child and his family and no suitable plan was developed for his treatment.

Within such a culture innovation is strongly discouraged. In fact, those brave workers who insist upon working in a manner that might prove helpful to individuals and families are challenged, as their mandate remains narrowly constrained. Innovation is essential to change. It requires creativity, risk taking, involvement of the community and the shattering of the silos. Sadly, professions and governments are averse to taking risks. Thus, when you squelch calculated risk taking, you wring creative thinking from those delivering the services. And without creative thinking, you suffocate innovation. This is not to say that there is no innovation right now. Whatever there is falls almost exclusively in the domain of voluntary-sector organizations. Throughout my career I've tried to be a risk taker and a creative thinker. The bottom line for me has been how we get the maximum effectiveness from our limited resources. This issue will be addressed in greater detail in a future chapter.

As noted earlier it seems to me that change can occur in two ways. Either you gradually change the system or you allow it to implode upon itself. It is important to note, however, that innovation is essential if change is going to occur. This point cannot be emphasized enough. Given that governments are averse to risk, there is little encouragement for doing things differently. Sadly, this leaves only one alternative — the implosion of the current social-program systems. As with the fall of communist countries, those most closely involved with day-to-day governance and administration rarely see the signs of pending implosion.

I am reminded of a group of four senior representatives of the Communist Youth Organization who visited Canada in 1962 to study Canadian youth programming. The national YMCA served as host. I received a call from the Y that the delegation wanted to visit with our detached street-work project. The reason for this interest, I soon learned from the delegation of four CYO leaders, was that the major cities of Russia were experiencing a rise in youth street-gang activity, something they hadn't seen since the early post-revolutionary years. I recall gathering my "boys" together at my apartment in the gang's local neighbourhood for an evening of discussion about our program. One of the members of the CYO group was a volunteer whose day job was that of professor of Canadian history at the University of Moscow. In discussion with him about his academic interest in Canada, I learned that Canada was an anomaly in Marxist political theory. We made the transition from colony to independence without a major revolution. At the time I was intrigued by the thought that Canada had been capable of making a major change without a violent upheaval. While it's a bit of a stretch, I am confident, based upon this story, that we are still capable of change. We don't require a revolution or the system's implosion to restore the directions we set for collective social programming. As was the case with our detached street-worker program, a remarkable service innovation in the early 1960s, we can still change our service directions through innovative programming. There are plenty of local examples that prove creative thinking still exists. Sadly, however, innovation is happening in spite of government and professional resistance to change, rather than because of encouragement and whole-hearted support.

We suffer from a deeply ingrained mindset. When we encounter human problems we simply throw more conventional services at the problem or issue. Therefore, if alcoholism is a problem, hire more addiction counsellors. When too many children are suffering abuse and neglect, hire more child-welfare personnel. And if people haven't enough to eat, create a food bank or soup kitchen. No one considers why substance abuse exists, why children are being neglected or abused in increasing numbers, or why people haven't got sufficient food to eat. We simply throw more services at the problems, hoping that matters will change for the better. Feedback suggests that things are not getting better as a result of spending more money for the provision of social services and programs.

If I were wrong, then the United States would have the healthiest population in the world. After all, the United States spends 13.9 percent of its GDP on health care and has one of the best doctor-to-population ratios in the world — 2.6 doctors for each 1,000 people. And yet citizens of the U.S. live to only age 76, three years less than the average Canadian. At the same time Canada spends only 9.2 percent of GDP and has a ratio of only 2.1 doctors to 1,000 people. And lest we get too content with ourselves, consider Japan, whose citizens live to age 80, a year longer than Canadians and four years longer than American citizens. Japan spends a frugal 7.1 percent of GDP on health care and has a miserly ratio of 1.7 doctors for every 1,000 of its citizens.

The point I am underscoring is that the health and well-being of communities bear little relationship to spending, though there's obviously a point when lack of spending does have extremely negative consequences upon health status and social well-being. Russia, as mentioned earlier, is a case in point. With a general decline in family income and reductions in health-care expenditures (now only 5.7 percent of GD), Russian health status has declined over the past decade. Russians can now count on living to only 67 years, 12 fewer years than the average Canadian.

At this point you're no doubt asking this question: "Come on, Couchman, if you're so insightful, what things can be done to solve this problem?" Thankfully there are some answers and there are already promising projects that demonstrate how we can do things better. I note, for example, that programs that have the support of participants as equal partners, whether they be youth, parents or community members, show more promising outcomes than programs where those being helped are not involved. That is to say, programs which do things with you, rather than for you, are generally more effective. Likewise, programs where collaboration occurs between service partners work best when the professionals and government departments stay within the comfortable confines of their respective silos. For example, implementing an education program that combines sensitivity to health, recreation and social needs of students from low-income families works far better than solely modifying the academic program.

One recent example of this is a project called the Whole Child Project, located at Whitehorse Elementary School in the Yukon. This project involves school personnel with parents and local professionals on an equal footing. While local school personnel and partner agencies struggled to obtain funding for the project, it wasn't until the national headquarters of the RCMP thought carefully about it that money was made available. The RCMP made a grant of $50,000 for the project's first year of operations and is now considering further funding for the second year. You must give the RCMP credit for thinking outside its highly structured box.

The project works with all elements of a child's life: learning, recreation, good nutrition and strong, nurturing family life. In other words, the child is loved by his or her family and respected by the community. This holistic approach governs how the services are offered to the child. Those involved are very "hands on," as they say. This often means that plenty of volunteer hours are given to the project. An RCMP constable, for example, runs an evening recreation program for the children in this inner-city community. As evening transportation for children is a problem due to severe cold in the north, the local Lion's Club donates the use of its van so that the constable can pick the children up at their homes and deliver them safe and warm at the end of the evening. A teacher runs a computer lab. A nutritionist offers a social evening for parents where they prepare a dinner. Meanwhile, down the hall the children enjoy a play group. In total, it's a warm and comprehensive approach to child development.

I'd like to say that the Whole Child Project is a highly innovative approach to healthy child development. It is not. Similar programs have been tried before with success. I, therefore, would place this little project in the category of common sense. The child is a learner, but he or she is also a social being, a much-loved son or daughter and a contributor to the community. To maximize potential the child must remain healthy, be physically active, loved and nurtured, be fed well, learn right from wrong and have his or her natural curiosity stimulated. In other words, the child is something more than his or her parts. It only makes sense that those who provide for the daily care, health, education and social well-being of the child should work together as they are working with a whole child, not isolated fragments of the child. The Whole Child Project is thus exquisitely simple. In the Whitehorse community, however, it is seen as highly innovative. It doesn't quite fit into the correct administrative box. As a result, the concept was viewed with trepidation by a number of bureaucrats who see their role as maintaining their respective boxes. The interests of children and families is an important but secondary consideration.

If you haven't worked in the field, you might wonder, at this point, how no one seems to have developed a policy that encourages such a sensible approach. I'm pleased to say that some government departments do have such a policy. As one example, the federal Ministry of Health has an approach that promotes health rather than simply seeing medical care as the sole factor in maintaining the health of Canadians. It considers those things that have been identified recently as determinants of health. As an illustration, we know that diet, exercise, a healthy environment, adequate sleep, close family life and adequate income keep people healthier and increase their longevity. Using this broad approach is one of the reasons Canadians do well in international comparisons of general health. When health policy is narrowly defined as simply "health care," outcomes, such as those referred to earlier, show little if any correlation between the amount of money we spend on health and our actual state of health. The number of doctors per capita, the amount of medical technology and the cost per hospital bed seem, within reason, to make absolutely no difference in how healthy we are as a society.

The Whole Child Project at Whitehorse Elementary School, like many similar approaches across the country, is successful because it considers as many human factors as possible in what makes for healthy children and healthy families. We talk these days about community capacity building. When you combine community resources and work in close partnership *with* people rather then doing things *for* people, you crack the silos wide open.

You can appreciate why I describe the Whole Child Project as common sense rather than as a startling innovation. One has to be really threatened to think that such a program is radical or risky. This, of course, is but one modest example of resistance to change and the impregnable nature of professional and government silos or stovepipes. My gosh, if this approach is viewed as a threat, you can understand how unsettling real innovation must be to those who govern our professions and human-care systems.

Unfortunately, the experience of school personnel in struggling to launch such a project is by no means an exception or unique. In fact, where innovation has been allowed to flourish, it has done so in spite of subtle, and often not-so-subtle, resistance from government or organizations heavily funded by government. Innovation requires an element of risk, and government is largely averse to taking risks. It also discourages the agencies it supports in taking risks, even when doing so promises far more effective results. In the past innovation was more readily embraced, as I recall from my days as a detached street worker. Of course, those were times of risk and innovation as both governments and people struggled to lay the cornerstones for social policy and services that did the job expected of them.

To change services and programs so that they do what they're supposed to do, major change is required. But change can only occur when innovation, I like to think of it as the social entrepreneurial spirit, is encouraged. You can't achieve innovation, of course, when you encounter professional protectionism, when you must work within fortress-like ministries and when agency survival is placed ahead of the quality of services. Innovation will not thrive until the internal culture supports creative thinking.

I have noted earlier in this work that the entire human-service system is highly resistant to change, despite compelling evidence that too many programs and services are either not working or are grossly unproductive. Change, even when it is for the better, is highly distressing to individuals who cherish stability and personal security above all else. But as I draw this conclusion, many readers will argue vehemently that they are aware of innovative programs being provided through a number of government departments and traditional agencies. Having been the director of several agencies, I am aware of this apparent contradiction in my argument. I respond by suggesting that if you scratch the veneer of this type of innovation, as mentioned several times in earlier chapters, you find that innovation's penetration is insignificant when it comes to creating fundamental change. Core programs remain the heart of most agencies, and the attention they give to innovative projects is, to say the least, superficial. The protective plating on core programs is extremely thick. In addition, core programs use up most of an organization's budget.

Innovation is like the frost on the cola can and the sizzle of the steak: we are being sold on the idea that the actual contents offer marvellous taste. Too often we find the cola less than expected and the steak too tough to enjoy. Innovation is like the frost on the tin. You're seduced into drinking the particular beverage, only to find that it's insipid. No, when I speak of innovation, I see a culture of creative thinking and real compassion running deep into the value system and behaviour of the organization or ministry. When innovation is used as window-dressing, it's not only dishonest but it prevents real change from occurring.

A number of years ago William White, the chairman of a large U.S. foundation, conducted a five-year follow-up study of innovative projects supported by his foundation. Much to his surprise he discovered that less than 10 percent of the projects remained in existence. While some innovation fails, White found that even those projects that were great successes no longer existed. When he inquired why this was the case, he was given the standard answer: "The funds ran out and we were unable to carry the program." Once he observed this phenomenon, he asked colleague foundations whether they were making the same observation. While few of them had conducted comprehensive follow-up studies, they discovered that similar patterns existed in the survival of innovative projects they had supported. Based upon this evidence, William White concluded that the several billion dollars spent on service innovation during the previous year had had little permanent impact on program development within the voluntary sector for that time period. In other words, the frost was on the tin and the sizzle in the steak, but the desire to change was a deliberate illusion. Like the Wizard of Oz working his machines behind the screen to create an illusion of power and authority, too much service innovation is simply smoke and mirrors.

To illustrate how this deliberate illusion looks on the ground, I recall my own frustration as a foundation president. In 1992 I received a call from a low-income parent who'd been involved in a self-help group operated by the London Middlesex Children's Aid Society. The mother described to me an excellent program for high-risk parents. During its two years of operation the program used a social-work facilitator from the agency, and no child of a parent involved within the group had to be taken into care. When I asked her why she called, she told me that she'd been advised to call me by agency management to seek further funding, as their innovative project grant had expired. "But," I said, "the cost of this program is minimal and the benefits enormous." She responded by telling me that she and the other low-income mothers had been advised by agency management that the society wasn't allowed to divert child-welfare money to its preventive project.

Alas, I had to decline the request, as our foundation was not in the business of being a substitute for government funding. I did, however, call the executive director and advise him that the agency should go to bat for these mothers. They shouldn't have to make cold calls to foundations. He wouldn't ask a frontline social worker to apply for a grant. Why then would his staff encourage a volunteer to undertake such fundraising? Unless, of course, staff members didn't see it as important in the overall scheme of things.

In her major research study of successful U.S. innovative programs for children, Dr. Lisbeth Schorr of Harvard University states that one of the qualities characterizing all successful programs is that "they owe their existence to idiosyncratic combinations of circumstances, talent and commitment that have prevailed in the face of the perverse incentives operating to discourage interventions of proven effectiveness."[1] She goes on in her book *Within Our Reach* to describe the project leaders as being "rebels" operating within their respective systems. They all seem to possess the skill of running interference for their workers and volunteers so that they can get on with the job at hand.

While I don't like to think that all service innovation is simply window-dressing, there seems ample evidence to suggest that innovation is being used as a vehicle to impress the public. No one likes to think that we're making so little progress in conquering the ills of society. However, many politicians, bureaucrats and managers are intransigent when it comes to seeking more positive outcomes. Resistance to change seems to serve as a systemic immune system to protect against program instability and personal insecurity. A host who insists upon maintaining such an immune system is likely to be on the road to extinction. Unless we alter course, the entire system will implode. While this may be a natural course, too many people will be hurt during the process of collapse and rebuilding. The challenge thus becomes the following: if we really care about people we'll change.

NOTES

---

1.   Lisbeth B. Schorr, *Within Our Reach* (New York: Anchor Books, 1989) p. 267.

Chapter 7

The Paradox
of
Accountability

Another of the three issues I began to consider is that of the bastardization of the principle of accountability. Like so many of my colleagues whose passion is creative program planning, I've tended to leave the subject of financial accountability to others within the organizations in which I've worked. I wouldn't go so far as to say I see financial accountability as a necessary evil. While I'd sooner sit in the dentist's chair than draft a budget, I acknowledge that sound financial management is an integral part of the role of a CEO. Accounting for how one spends resources, however, doesn't equate to measuring the effectiveness of the work that is done with individuals, families and the community.

In the private sector a manager receives immediate feedback if the company's goods or services are not selling. In a social agency, however, feedback on the quality of the services is neither direct nor immediate. Thus, the health and vitality of the organization may not show up in the bottom line. In fact, some of the most effective social and health organizations may be struggling with their bottom lines simply because of their desire to go the extra mile for the people with whom they work. As is frequently the case, in fact, good agencies never seem to have sufficient financial resources. They are always stretching themselves.

In terms of how accountability is measured, however, so long as rates of production and number of people served meet some amorphous standard known to officials of government or other funding sources, the funder seems satisfied. Little attention is paid to whether the services and programs are actually helping the clients or patients served by these organizations. Even the use of the words "client" and "patient" suggests to me an inappropriate concept. Someone to whom things are done is called a client. Someone who is served is called a customer. The term customer possesses a sense of reciprocity unknown to the terms "client" or "patient."

As I say, I certainly understand the rationale for maintaining financial accountability. When you are administering public funds, whether they be donations or tax dollars, you must adhere to rigorous standards of responsibility. In my work over the years I certainly had no trouble with this important principle. Every year the reckoning would occur, the board meeting at which the final financial results of the last year's operations were reviewed. Following this exercise the budget would be set for next year's operations. Once again, directors, many of whom come from the private sector, would give the figures and projections close attention. Over time, however, it began to dawn on me that similar attention was not being given to the results and outcomes of our services and programs. In my simple mind accountability is a balanced equation. Financial resources occur on one side of the equation and the other side is balanced by results or outcomes. In most instances numbers of clients seen or interviews offered suffice to meet the expectations of government. In addition, one might be asked to evaluate program activities, usually a highly subjective enterprise.

When dealing with money it's easy to add up figures, undergo an audit or offer reasonable comfort to a spender. After all, the minimum expectation of the funders is that their money is spent in accordance with service agreements and within the approved budget. What this exercise seriously lacks, however, is any sense as to whether your services and programs are improving the health, education and social well-being of people.

In my early years in the 1960s and 1970s funding of the human-care system was greatly restrained. Even taking into account rising operating costs, what was being spent on family counselling, for example, when I came to the Family Service Association of Metro Toronto in 1974 was a pittance of the operating costs of the agency during my final year in 1989. In 14 years the budget went from $3 million to more than $8 million. The same scenario was also played out in education, health care and other fields of human service. Interestingly, this generous change in expenditures occurred at a time when the baby-boom cohort began to take on administrative responsibilities for corporate, government and voluntary-sector systems.

With the frugal mindset I inherited from the deprivation experienced by my family and neighbourhood during the Great Depression and the war years, I was taken aback by the new attitudes toward spending. It's safe to say, however, that I was just as seduced by the largess as anyone. Like most others, I had little sense of the connectivity between the dollars flowing into my agency and the mounting federal deficit. But let me jump ahead of myself.

As I've said, financial accountability is a very positive value. The fact that it was taking on a larger-than-life profile at a time when social policy was being significantly reduced should have been seen as a matter for concern. During the era of early development of the Canadian welfare state, social, health and education policies were significant influences in shaping new services and programs. Those were the days, of course, when the Canada Assistance Plan closely governed the development of welfare-state programs. The plan, which cost-shared social programs between provinces and territories and our federal government, set out clear parameters for both essential services and those services deemed to be worthy of enhancements.

The Constitution of Canada gave provinces direct responsibility for the operation of social programs. On the other hand, the federal government dictated what programs they would cost share. It was sort of a check-and-balance approach and worked reasonably well, as it provided social equity from one province or territory to the next. Thus, no matter where you lived in Canada, you could be assured that your basic needs would be met. In this way, certain national standards were set and maintained. The arrangement provided an effective dual system of financial accountability. The weakness of the arrangement, however, was that the Canada Assistance Plan offered little flexibility to provinces. Those provinces that wished to do more for their citizens were denied federal cost sharing. Because of the static nature of the Canada Assistance Plan, another subtle problem was to enter the picture. Those who wished to be more innovative in the delivery of their social and health programs were discouraged from doing so.

To appease the provinces and to eliminate an area of federal-provincial friction, the federal government made the decision to block-fund provinces for their social-service and health programs. As a result, what had been a sound dual system of accountability became a linear system. With the exception of health care, which maintained certain national standards, social services were placed almost solely into the hands of provincial governments, and more recently in the hands of territorial governments.

I well recall going to the ramparts on this issue at an Ottawa meeting of the Canadian Council on Social Development. Despite the friction and a clear need to reform the Canada Assistance Plan, most of my colleagues were very worried that social-service programs in less enlightened provinces would be decimated. This, in fact, occurred in several provinces as social services were no longer a priority. Block funding, while a comfortable political solution for the federal government, proved to be much less advantageous to the public, in the hands of many provincial governments.

This is sufficient background to understand the underlying crisis in accountability that arose from the funding adjustment. In just about every locale across Canada, thoughtful social policy analysis and development were relegated to the back rooms of provincial ministries responsible for social services.

In one instance I was asked to deliver a training workshop for the policy analysts of one major provincial social-service ministry. Sensing that the group seemed quite demoralized, I made the comment that it must be difficult to work in a setting where a year of your work could be readily tossed in a wastepaper basket. At that point I think I said that it's at least some comfort to see that about 20 percent of your work is being taken seriously. Then a loud voice came from the back of the room: "Try five percent." Immediately the deputy minister jumped up and requested that the speaker identify himself. No one rose and the DM, thinking better about pushing the matter further, decided not to ask the assembled civil servants who had made the comment. Given the mood in the room it was obvious that the group would have simply closed ranks in support of the anonymous critic. As I recall, the workshop went downhill from there.

The vacuum left by the diminishing of policy was quickly filled by political ideology from both the right and the left. Many governments shifted to program development by public polling and the personal intervention of influential constituents. Without accurate knowledge, priorities could not be objectively set, and an already complex area of program development turned into a quagmire of competing special interests. In such a climate it's little wonder that serious social problems such as hunger, homelessness, alienated youth, child poverty and inadequate support services for the mentally ill and mentally challenged were placed on the back burner. Far more acceptable groups of "deserving" people were much more adept at commanding attention.

In my mind one of the best illustrations of the contrast between "deserving" and "undeserving" recipients of public largess occurred while I was president of the Donner Canadian Foundation. The board of the foundation liked to treat its volunteer directors well. As a result, we often met in quite sumptuous settings. On this particular weekend the board meeting was to be held at the Breakers Hotel in Palm Beach, Florida. I recall driving to the entrance of the hotel that evening to find a long line of high-end luxury cars discharging well-dressed patrons at the door. When my turn came to turn the vehicle over to the attendant, I asked what special function was occurring in the ballroom that evening. I was informed that it was a public benefit ball. Having witnessed so many homeless people sleeping in doorways in West Palm Beach as I drove from the airport, I was cheered to think that the wealthy residents of Palm Beach were hosting an event in favour of a local charity. The next day I heard from one of the hotel attendants that the ball, attended by 500 guests, had raised more money than any similar fundraising event in U.S. history.

The total raised was a staggering $18 million. Needless to say, being a Canadian, I was in shock. I asked "what charity was to be the beneficiary of this large amount of money." It turned out that the funds raised that evening were for a new performing arts centre for the residents of Palm Beach. While I could not be critical of people lending such support to the arts, I was stunned to learn that these funds were being matched by support from both the U.S. and Florida governments. And the poor of West Palm Beach still sleep in doorways.

Though this is an American example, it speaks all too eloquently to the evolution of self-interest as a basis for establishing social-program priorities. During the Middle Ages the poor of the parish, largely widows and orphans, qualified as deserving. The vagabonds and poor male out-siders were labelled undeserving and quickly encouraged to leave town. Today it's safe to say that homeless individuals, those who have insuffi-cient food to eat and those who are on welfare are the undeserving poor.

An objective assessment of need has little place in setting a rational and humane policy framework for social-security and social-services programs. This is not to say that some programs for the so-called unde-serving underclass are not being funded. Having homeless people beg-ging on the streets is a highly visible and uncomfortable inconvenience. Thus, there is enough public support to pressure most governments into taking some action. When this action is taken, it is generally announced with public fanfare. The funds provided, however, represent a small percentage of what is actually required to solve the problem.

This can be compared with the eradication of serious poverty among seniors back in the 1980s. There is not a senior today who is less well-off than a poverty-level family with children. Of course, children are not voters and they lack the same public appeal as seniors.

The most common current viewpoint, behind the ranking of social security and social services, is the sense that welfare recipients should get out and work like everyone else. There are certainly a number of people who take advantage of welfare, and the current structure may well act as a disincentive for some people who are capable of holding down a minimum-wage job. This, however, is not the case among the majority of welfare recipients whom I've encountered over the years. Most were all too anxious to regain their financial independence. However, it seems to serve us well to have public scapegoats to justify our choice of spending priorities.

To this point I've argued that accountability is an equation: money goes in one side and things happen for the poor, disabled, etc. on the other side. I've also taken pains to note the decimation of the analysis role and policy-development specialists within departments and min-istries of government. For a number of years I pondered the question of whether this decimation made much of a difference in how effective we were at actually helping people. How could we help people without thoughtful direction from government? Then one day at the University of Chicago in 1992, the danger hit me full force.

I was attending a conference that was reviewing a research study comparing U.S. social programs with those of Canada. The project was sponsored jointly by Canada's Fraser Institute and the University of Chicago. Gary Becker served as chair for the gathering and was soon to become a Nobel Prize winner in economics. Gathered around the table sat some of North America's top economists. Their task was to review the cost effectiveness of social programs, comparing Canada with the United States. Fair enough, I thought, our systems should be able to stand up to this rigorous accountability review. Then it happened; one of the economists indicated that in his piece of the comparative study, his research team had noted that increasing welfare rates seemed to increase the potential for family breakdown. This finding was carefully noted and general agreement was quickly achieved. Higher welfare rates were bad for family unity. As the only person in the room with a background in social science, I was stunned at this simplistic analysis. I then looked about the room and noted that the only women in attendance were senior graduate students from the economics department of the university. They were seated at the back of the room as observers.

I knew that to argue against this finding with an impressive group of economists would be futile. The correlation between increased welfare rates and family breakdown was a matter of fact. Then it dawned on me. In a study of marriage breakdown among clients of the Family Service Association of Metro Toronto, I had noted that the chances of marital separation increased among women with higher education. As one might expect, the greatest risk of separation occurred among women with less than secondary school education. On the other hand, those women with secondary school graduation diplomas seemed to have quite stable marriages. My simple study went on to show that women with B.A.s had slightly less stability in their marriages. However, women with master's degrees and doctorates experienced relationships almost as unstable as women with less than secondary school educations, the Ph.D.s having the greatest risk of separation and divorce.

I outlined my observations to the group and then posed a question. Graduate studies seemed to appreciably increase the chances that a woman would separate or divorce her partner. Consistent with the consensus view that it might be better to keep welfare rates low in the name of family unity, should we not discourage women from entering graduate school? Suddenly, I noted, the female graduate students were listening carefully for a response. There was a long, thoughtful silence. Then Gary Becker said, greatly to my relief, "You've got an excellent point there.

Perhaps we should exercise caution in how much we extrapolate from our economic studies." As the example illustrates, there is a danger in using a single lens for the development of social policy. Human problems are much more complex than a single academic discipline can fathom. For me, this example also spoke, once again, to the need to bring together academic disciplines and professionals from various fields. I suspect that if I'd not intervened, the published findings of this study between the Fraser Institute and the University of Chicago might have been used by legislators as justification for maintaining welfare rates well below the poverty line. Family stability, while an extremely important social issue, is not everything, as the young women at the back of the room realized.

Sad to say, over time this corrupted version of the concept of accountability further damaged the delivery of social services. By placing financial accountability into the prime position, you created an unbalanced equation. Considering the impact of this way of measuring service effectiveness, I now realize that we squeezed out any incentive for frontline workers to take risks and find better ways of working with people. Their principal task was to spend within their allocated budgets and produce maximum numbers of service units. Ensuring the effectiveness of their work became secondary. In fact, it became so secondary that you were foolhardy to think creatively and take risks. Thank God, however, so many compassionate workers remain foolhardy.

As a sad example of the unbalanced accountability equation, consider what happened to a friend of ours. For years our friend suffered from increasingly debilitating MS. Now confined to bed and her electric wheelchair, it had become necessary for her to receive attendant home care. When the Department of Social Services was told that its budget was being reduced by five percent, management decided to pass the problem on to its service supervisors: "We don't know how you'll do it, but reduce your operating budgets by five percent." In turn, the supervisors passed on the problem to their home-care workers by increasing their caseloads five percent. Thus, the frontline workers were expected to come up with their own solutions. A very frustrated and demoralized home-care attendant visited our friend and asked whether she thought that one bath a week, instead of three, would suffice. The worker, confronted by directives from head office, saw little other recourse. If she was to provide all her clients, including the new ones added to her caseload, with basic care, such a step had to be taken. Our friend could feel the anguish this worker was feeling as she came up against the wall of responsible financial accountability.

This illustration is by no means unique. As I write this chapter an elderly couple and their severely retarded son are being buried in the province of British Columbia because the B.C. Ministry of Family and Children's Services refused to provide the family with the $500 a month that would have gone to son if he'd been living on his own. This little bit of money would have helped to defray the financial losses the family experienced as its savings dipped to zero. Seeing no hope, the boy's father hooked the exhaust pipe of his vehicle to a hose and the members of the family voluntarily took their own lives rather than see the dignity of their simple lives destroyed. I am not condoning their decision. I am just illustrating how estranged service accountability has become from financial accountability. The latter is being closely embraced with religious fervour, while the quality of the former is being deeply discounted.

In his book *Voltaire's Bastards*, John Ralston Saul explains that those French civil servants who were disciples of Voltaire's system of rational logic were required, before implementing their policies, to ask themselves, "Does this make sense?" If not, they were to go back and re-examine their logic to see what flaw had occurred.[1] When you eliminate or castrate your policy analysts, as has occurred in the federal government and in many provincial and municipal governments, the question "Does this make sense?" no longer gets asked.

The loss of service flexibility is thus the most destructive consequence sacrificed at the high altar of financial accountability. In my estimation, the decimation of objective social-policy analysis virtually destroys the vision and intent of the architects who put in place Canada's first government-supported social programs.

Perhaps the most bizarre and telling illustration of corrupted accountability occurred as recently as December 2, 2001. I was attending a meeting of the Regulatory Table of Custom and Revenue on Canada's Voluntary Sector Initiative. At the time we were struggling with the issue of financial accountability in terms of which voluntary-sector organizations should be given permission to issue tax receipts. As a voluntary-sector representative sitting on the table, I was attempting to come to grips with why one of my charitable gifts should be recognized as a tax deduction and another charitable gift should receive no special tax treatment. As I have come to believe, my donations are a personal decision that I make with respect to supporting worthy causes and organizations. My gifts are after-tax dollars, though I may receive modest relief if I give to a registered charity.

At this point in the discussion the representative from the Department of Finance expressed the opinion that all personal income generously and freely offered by citizens as donations rightfully belongs to Finance. His argument, as I followed it, was that any dollar given as a charitable gift was a dollar taken away from the treasury of Canada. Following the logic of this viewpoint, my personal giving is actually being offered at the sufferance of the Canadian Department of Finance. Naturally, if I was to receive a 100 percent tax deduction, this would be the case. However, if I am using my own money to strengthen the social, cultural or environmental fabric of my country, the Government of Canada should take great delight in my generosity. In too many instances I am offering personal gifts to causes and issues for which government should be responsible (e.g., assistance to the homeless, food for the poor, care for the elderly, etc.). With such distorted thinking on the part of the Department of Finance, it is little wonder that accountability has become totally linear.

It may well be, of course, that the arguments being raised by my table colleague from Finance are not an accurate reflection of the Government of Canada's official position. I did note, however, that none of the other senior civil servants around the table chose to disagree with their Finance colleague's interpretation. I therefore left the meeting feeling that the stated position is an accurate reflection of current government thinking.

I can see senior government recoiling at my interpretation of events and actions. After all, they will argue, the effectiveness of our services is equal to financial accountability. All government rhetoric would have us believe that this is true. In fact, statement after statement is issued to this effect in government documents and in speeches by our elected representatives. However, if this were true, would you not find government totally embracing the need for proper program evaluation?

Some time ago I was invited, as a foundation president, to sit on a panel of funders at a conference for those professionals working in the field of program evaluation. My provincial and federal counterparts on the panel spoke in detail about the importance of evaluating services and programs contracted out by governments. At that point in the proceedings, as the panel began the dialogue among its members, I asked my federal and provincial panel counterparts to tell us how they evaluate programs run directly by the government. There was a moment's silence, some nervous throat clearing and the federal member on the panel said that government did not have to evaluate the effectiveness of its own programs. He did add, of course, that the federal programs, such as employment insurance, were subject to scrupulous financial audit. And we certainly know about that, I thought to myself.

For a government to take the matter of accountability seriously, it must not only insist that those programs receiving government grants undergo proper evaluations, it must also have its own work evaluated by objective external evaluators. In my opinion, many of the existing ideologically derived policies do not stand the test of objective analysis. Thus, I have to sadly conclude that far too many current social-policy practices are the result of fallacious thinking and planning. When it comes to taking service effectiveness seriously, program evaluation becomes a universal requirement and the results are used to adjust programs so that they can become more effective.

I began this chapter by suggesting that accountability is no longer seen as a balanced equation. On the one side are financial resources. On the other side are program outcomes. Not only must we be accountable for the dollars spent on social, health, education and cultural programs, but we owe it to the Canadian people, particularly those people we serve, to ensure that our efforts are efficient and effective. Most important of all, we should create an open culture in which creativity and innovation are welcome and, in fact, celebrated. Sure, mistakes will be made. They are in every area of creative human endeavour. To start with, we must take a simple initial step, that of allowing frontline workers to undertake compassionate flexibility on behalf of the people with whom they work. It makes sense, so that's a place to start.

NOTES

1. John Ralston Saul, *Voltaire's Bastards: The Dictatorship of Reason in the West* (Toronto: Penguin Books of Canada, 1992).

Chapter 8

The Dynamic
of
Canadian Character

During the last two chapters I've looked at the factors that have worked against the social-welfare state in the past couple of decades. The isolationist mentality of professions and governments as well as the bastardization of the concept of accountability are simply the mechanics of what went wrong. There must be, I thought, something beyond the physical mismanagement of the social-service systems that challenges us to question our systems of collective social responsibility. Probe as I might for further errors in the system, I was unable to come up with anything beyond variations on the two issues of silo mentalities and corrupted accountability.

It took some time before I considered that the mechanics of how we deliver social programs have been accompanied by a dramatic sociocultural change in Canadian character. Did the decline in the mechanics of the social-welfare system, combined with annual budget deficits, link in any way with this change in Canadian character?

Like those I write about, I had been thinking inside a box. Being a professional and the frequent head of several major social-service organizations, I, too, was encumbered by the same narrow mindset as my colleagues and government bureaucrats. If the social-welfare state was brought into being because of the collective concern of Canadians in the 1920s and 1930s, might it be possible to look at character as a significant factor in both the rise and decline of the welfare state? In retrospect this seemed an all-too-evident explanation as to why Canadians were unable to correct the mechanical problems within the system when they became very clear. On this basis I concluded that national character is the single most influential factor in shaping Canadian social programs.

Canada is, of course, not isolated when it comes to character formation. Throughout the Western world we have witnessed a change in national character in all countries that have embraced the concept of collective social responsibility. As with common structural or mechanical flaws in the operation of the welfare state, national character contributed in no small way to the present state of affairs. It is essential, therefore, to recognize that the design and operation of social programs are done against a backdrop of national character.

While we may not always be able to define the specifics of national culture, which is the birthplace of character, it's nevertheless the most powerful influence imaginable in shaping our collective attitudes and values. It was out of experiences like my mother's cardboard soles, the hobos coming to the back door for food and the bitter indignity of being on the dole that Canadians concluded, "Enough is enough." Unemployment insurance, medicare and family allowances thus had their roots in Canadian determination. We must look after one another. It's on the basis of these values and attitudes that all social programs were developed.

National character gives rise to spiritual, moral and even political directions. Canada was founded, for example, on the constitutional principles of peace, order and good government. It is also no accident that peace, order and good government came to define a major portion of our national character. The national character of Canadians, even during the formative colonial years, was to protect minority groups within the country, even when this involved sacrifices with respect to preserving the freedom of the individual.

In the United States the constitution was developed with the rights and freedoms of the individual as a central pillar for governance. As a result of embracing a classic liberal ideology, our U.S. neighbours developed social programs as a bit of an afterthought. This does not mean that the U.S. simply threw its widows and orphans and the disabled to the wolves. Inherent in the religious character of Americans was the imperative of personal generosity. In fact, in the early years of the country charity was not simply a personal choice, it was a moral imperative set down by churches. Today Americans are among the most generous personal givers in the world. American foundations, for example, give out $100 a year for every dollar distributed by a Canadian foundation. If the ratio were based upon population, it would be $10 to $1. Given the quality of personal generosity within the American character, it's frankly a surprise to find that they have any national social programs or social security. Had it not been for Franklin Delano Roosevelt's New Deal, implemented during the Great Depression, the contemporary United States might have even weaker social security than it does today.

Canada, however, found its cultural roots in royalist and conservative traditions, with government being seen as essential for civil stability. As Canadians we also found ourselves in a much harsher climate and more demanding geography than our southern American neighbours. According to Margaret Atwood, we hunkered down against the climatic elements rather than feeling that cold weather and our geography were something we could conquer. At the core of American character is the theme of conquering the wilderness and other natural forces. Thankfully for Americans, they live under far more naturally benign conditions than we do in Canada. Rather than be rugged individualists, we must pull together just to survive.

Canadians, therefore, came to depend on family and neighbours for their comfort and survival, rather than standing as individuals capable of conquering the frontier. Social anthropologists feel that this may explain the collective concern that Canadians have for one another's welfare. It's an interesting observation to note that most northern countries also place collective welfare ahead of personal independence. For example, some of the strongest socialized states in the world are found in Scandinavia. Russia, with one of the harshest northern climates, also came to embrace a radical form of socialism. While I don't want to push this analysis too far afield, it's interesting to note the physical/political parallels.

Recently old Joe, who lives with a few shaggy highland cows up the Surprise Lake Road east of Atlin, had his house burn down in the middle of the night. He of course wasn't insured, but all his belongings were destroyed. He spent the remainder of a very frosty night in his cowshed. Within hours the community was mobilized to help Joe. Whether you liked reclusive Joe or not, he was a neighbour and therefore you were compelled to assist him. That's what neighbours do, particularly in frontier communities. Within hours Joe was re-outfitted, provided with food, a little cash and a neighbourly commitment to help him rebuild.

A contrasting anecdote occurred to me a couple of winters back. I was driving the Atlin Road, a 102-kilometre stretch of wilderness road connecting Atlin to the Alaska Highway. The temperature that morning hovered at a bone-chilling −30°C. Coming round a bend in the road, I saw a car stuck in the ditch. I immediately pulled over, went to the trunk and took out my shovel, and proceeded back to the car, which had spun into about three feet of snow. I noted the driver began to cower. I asked him if he wanted a hand. He hesitantly said yes, but continued to keep a sharp eye on me and the sharp spade slung over my shoulder. In the end I discovered the cause for his fear. He was a film producer from Los Angeles and thought the bearded fellow approaching him was going to kill him and discard his body in this wild and remote place. In appreciation he offered to feature me in the bagel commercial he was about to film in Atlin. I thanked him and said I had business to attend to in Whitehorse. He was certainly surprised with my response and assured me that the spot would pay well. I happily continued north on the Atlin Road to Whitehorse.

I cite these two stories to illustrate the social solidarity that Canadians feel toward each other. Whether the Saguenay or Red River is in flood, an ice storm disables a region or a fire destroys a seniors' residence, Canadians continue to do what neighbours in Canada have always done. It's a deep-rooted part of our national character. And so when those suffering illness or accident are in need, Canadians are happy that they support a national medicare program. In fact, medicare remains one of the major social programs that strongly unites all Canadians. Though we worry about its quality and are willing to consider other options, there is no public support for embracing an American-style system of health care. The

U.S. system, at last count, leaves close to 45 million Americans without health-care insurance. That would not be tolerated in Canada. It's not a neighbourly policy.

Canadian social programs in their various forms were developed as a means of ensuring that those in greatest need within our society receive the care and attention they deserve as citizens. "In that you have done unto the least of these my brethren, you have done it unto me." This commandment from Christ has been a pillar of personal responsibility toward the poor, the sick and the disabled throughout our history. Similar ethical principles are shared among other of the world's great religions, and many of these predate Christ. For Canadians, however, social obligation became both a personal responsibility and a collective responsibility, both driven by a moral imperative.

We often rationalize the problem of contrasting values away. "If only government had the political will to reflect our values," we often say. Of course, government may simply be reflecting those societal values that embarrass us and make us feel guilty. In his book *The Ingenuity Gap*, Thomas Homer-Dixon writes, "What we complacently identify as a lack of political will is in reality a lack of social will: we are all part of the problem, and our societies as a whole, not just our leaders, are ineffective in providing solutions to the challenges we face."[1] There is little more to add to this criticism except to say that once upon a time society possessed the social will to overcome government resistance and lethargy. It can be done again if we muster our collective social will.

So far I've provided an overly simplified explanation for the sociocultural roots of Canadian character. I'm sure my academic friends could write several volumes on the subject. When one looks at how character influences personal behaviour and social policy, however, there's a leap of faith between the concept of personal generosity and collective generosity. Both, nevertheless, have their origins in character. As we've seen from my Canadian/U.S. comparison, the people of both nations have a strong inclination toward personal generosity. In Canada our sense of collective responsibility paralleled our sense of personal obligation. This is a distinction between Canadians and our neighbours south of the border. At some point in time Canadians came to the realization that groups of its citizens were falling through the limited generosity of personal giving.

As we know, personal charitable giving is highly selective. The further one gets away from the cause requiring our financial compassion, the less likely it is that we will give money. Who, for example, is one's neighbour? Are they the victims of a serious mishap in Quebec, the far north or on the parched Prairies? Canadians, who drew their collective character from the harshness of an unforgiving land, recognized in the formative years of our history that neighbours are every minority group suffering serious personal hardship in every corner of the country. Our political roots in peace, order and good government became the expression of our national character.

It's relevant here to note an important finding of the Canadian Institute for Advanced Research. The Institute concluded from its studies that countries that thrive and succeed have two essential characteristics. First of all, the country must have a productive economy and, secondly, there must be a strong sense of reciprocal obligation among its people. It's obvious from the economic success of the United States that it has an extremely productive economy. This success is not, however, balanced by a strong sense of reciprocal obligation insofar as collective social programs are concerned. For the past several years the United Nations has included Canada among the top three countries in the world as far as standard of living is concerned. The U.S., on the other hand, has generally ranked in the top 10, but has never exceeded Canada's ranking. The fact that Canada developed strong social-welfare programs has a lot to do with our general standard of living exceeding that of Americans.

The momentum for the transition from personal obligation to collective responsibility occurred as a result of a fundamental character distinction. Canada was a country that abolished slavery soon after the American Revolution, thanks to the leadership of Nova Scotians and leaders like Governor John Graves Simcoe of Upper Canada. Though it took until the anti-slavery bill passed in England in 1834 to officially eliminate slavery throughout the Empire, Canada had by that time not practised slavery in many years. This choice reflects our respect for the rights of minority groups. In a country that cherishes the rights of the individual to maintain personal property and profit from it, the elimination of slavery demanded a high human sacrifice.

It's of interest to note that the first black invited to attend a social function at the White House was a man named Doctor Ruffin Abbott.

Abbott, who was a Canadian surgeon trained at Trinity College in Toronto, served as a volunteer with the Union Army. Abbott became a friend of Lincoln's after one of the more devastating battles of the Civil War. Lincoln came across Abbott in a field, inland close to the battlefield, and they walked together for more than two hours in thoughtful conversation with one another. This is not to idealize Canadian character. Bigotry and intolerance cannot be eliminated by official edict. Such attitudes and behaviours exist to this day through-out Canada. What is noteworthy, however, is that collective social responsibility carried the day. Alas, personal bigotry, hatred and self-centredness still exist in abundance within Canada. What is significant to note is that they are not seen as acceptable attitudes and behaviours by the body politic.

It was against this historic cultural backdrop that the seeds for the Canadian welfare state were sown. It took the devastating occurrence of the Great Depression, however, to translate the solidarity of social con-cern into actual legislation and programs. The last hurdle was the deep-seated conviction on the part of the majority of citizens that personal social and economic misfortunes were products of sloth and deliberate ignorance. The sands of the Western dust bowl blew into the faces of those convinced that severe poverty was a chosen personal state. Likewise, the number of young men eager to find any form of produc-tive labour ran contrary to popular belief about poverty. The dichoto-my between so-called deserving poor (largely widows, orphans and the physically disabled) and the undeserving poor (just about everyone else) gave ground to reasoned observation as most Canadians acknowl-edged that the line separating deserving from undeserving poor is blurred. Undoubtedly, this realization gave the concept of universality a real boost. If programs become universal, it really doesn't matter whether you are apparently deserving or undeserving. Sadly, as we can see from hungry children and the homeless in our streets, it didn't quite work out this way. Universality was bastardized with the change in Canadian character from a sense of personal reciprocal obligation to a collective sense of entitlement.

Of course, no group was more down on itself than those unem-ployed persons whose families were forced to rely on the dole. Like everyone else in Canadian society, their values and character had been shaped by a firm belief in the dignity of work and economic independence. This is an extremely important value in Canadian character. The architects of unemployment insurance understood this completely and realized that social welfare, in its several forms, would only be sought as a last resort and then with heavy hearts and reluctance. As we will see later in this chapter, this collective characteristic was to change in the 1960s and 1970s.

"In that you have done this unto the least of these my brethren ye have done it unto me." These words gave inspiration to a small group of clergy in Western Canada under the rubric of the social gospel. The likes of James Woodsworth, Tommy Douglas and Stanley Knowles believed that God's kingdom could be established on earth. In their minds the greatest social democrat in history was Jesus. Thus, they moved seamlessly from the pulpit to the floor of the House of Commons, where they badgered the Liberal government to enact social reforms to alleviate the suffering of the poor.

Woodsworth's first success came in 1927 with the passing of an act governing pensions for the elderly, many of whom became destitute after their retirement. There were few company pension plans at that time. The Great Depression, however, was a much greater threat to social stability. It had become obvious to all that far too many eager and hard-working Canadians were walking the streets or riding the rails in search of employment. Both the Conservative and Liberal governments were under constant attack by Woodsworth's crew of social democrats. Also contributing to the cause were external organizations like the United Church of Canada, the Neighbourhood Workers Association of Toronto and the Canadian Congress of Labour. Despite growing public support for state-sponsored social programs, government's greatest fear was that communism was growing in popularity among the dispossessed. If anything would upset social stability, it would be an uprising inspired by communist instigators. The Regina Riot was all too fresh in the minds of parliamentarians; hence, they realized something had to be done before chaos ruled. And one thing a government founded on the principles of peace, order and good government doesn't want is social chaos.

Parliamentarians were also aware that the deeply rooted Canadian value of looking after one's neighbours was becoming a significant political force throughout the country. Thus, in 1940 the first Unemployment Insurance Act was passed by Mackenzie King's Liberal government. Though a little late to be of much help to the unemployed, it offered assurance that, should another economic disaster befall Canadian families, some modest protection could be provided.

The past chapters have dealt primarily with Canada's social history during the past 62 years. Of course, character is something that spans even more generations. One theory that helps us understand how values and attitudes cross generations is offered by the American social historian Elise Boulding. Boulding developed the concept of the 200-year presence. According to her theory, the lives of our great great-grandparents or great-grandparents, born 100 years ago, still exert an influence on our character development. Likewise, our lives will shape the lives of our great great-grandchildren or great-grandchildren 100 years hence. This interpretation of the 200-year presence is a personal one. Take, for example, my grandmother, who passed on her compassion to my mother, who in turn passed the same value on to me. I have little doubt that their character strongly influenced my career directions. Had my grandmother been an accountant and my mother a businessperson, I suspect that I would have chosen a different career path, as well as have more money in my bank account.

I would suggest, as well, that the concept of the 200-year presence can be applied to the development of our collective character. In fact, the influence is felt much further back than 100 years, as I illustrated earlier in this chapter.

Character, however, is subject to change, particularly when social, economic and cultural conditions are in a state of flux. During the Middle Ages, for example, the economy and social conditions changed very little for several hundred years. The specific character of people living in various regions was not subject to a great deal of change and so remained much the same. In fact, we still live with many of the stereotypes that evolved during periods of chronic equilibrium. The romantic tendency of the French, Italians and Spanish, the diligence of the Dutch, the independent work ethic of Americans, the temper and moroseness of the Irish and the tendency of Canadians to maintain spaces that are safe and clean: these are but a few examples.

The fact is that few of these national characteristics are the same today as they were 300 or even 100 years earlier. During the industrial and post-industrial revolutions, and during the recent high-tech information-age revolution, tastes changed, culture changed, personal economic circumstances changed and, subsequently, public attitudes changed. A consequence of these changes was a major change in national character. I'm not saying, as too many nostalgic old farts would say, "Let's return to more ideal times." By any objective measure those times were not ideal. In fact, there was far more personal suffering during the 1930s and 1940s than we experience today, despite a greater tendency on the part of people during that era to help their extended families and neighbours. On the other hand, not all changes are necessarily positive. Canadians, for example, gradually lost their hearty sense of self-respect in terms of seeing unemployment insurance and social assistance as programs of last resort. A simple system designed to meet basic human needs under short-term, exceptional financial circumstances swiftly became seen as universal entitlement. It was this change in character that was to bring down the social-welfare system on our heads.

It was this sense of entitlement that forced governments to place more and more money into the social-welfare envelope. The argument, used by those who promoted and still promote universality, is that everyone needs to believe in social programs. The reasoning is that if everyone benefits, no one will be anxious to eliminate the programs. Those who were involved in social planning also identified the need to eliminate the social stigma attached to receiving benefits on the basis of a means test. While this goal was certainly a worthy one, it opened the door for expenditures that rapidly outstripped resources.

In her book *The Wealthy Banker's Wife*, Linda McQuaig makes the point that even people who don't need the support of Canadian social programs feel an entitlement to public largess.[2] Of course, McQuaig's primary argument is that there is a certain amount of greed going on within the system. Her identification of this characteristic is perhaps the most profound observation she makes. By the late 1970s greed replaced the founding principle of aid for individuals and families under exceptional circumstances.

I know that one always thinks of his or her best arguments after the fact. However, if I were to have my discussion of December 2, 2001, with my colleague from the federal Department of Finance again, I would underscore the point that my charitable dollars go directly to those who are disadvantaged or suffering from some physical or mental challenge. Tax dollars, over which I have little control once they are in the treasury, are dedicated in large portion to Canadians who don't require assistance.

Nowhere is the argument better illustrated then in the provision of care to the homeless. Few people ask themselves, "If we are giving so much of our tax dollar to support social-security services, how is it that I see so much absolute human destitution around me?" The answer is embarrassingly simple. Homeless people do not have a permanent place of residence; therefore you cannot send them a welfare cheque. Of course, the wealthy banker's wife does have a permanent address, so for years she received a family allowance cheque and still receives certain universal tax benefits.

I have had the argument on the merits and problems inherent in a system of universal social programs with colleagues and friends for many years. They argue, often quite vehemently, that universality rids the stigma from the receipt of social programs. This, as I said earlier, makes the programs acceptable to all Canadians. At an intellectual level I understand this rationale. What I find extremely distressing, however, is that many of the same advocates of the principle of universality give little attention to those in very serious need. It's interesting to note that those demanding we help homeless people, that we feed children, that we give high-quality care to the physically and mentally challenged are ordinary citizens. Yes, there are a number of social workers, health-care personnel and teachers in the ranks, but they constitute a minority. Rarely, by the way, do they have the whole-hearted support of the organizations and institutions for which they work. Nevertheless, they are an articulate and vocal minority and I take my hat off to them, which is a real tribute when it's −30°C much of the time during our Yukon winters.

If my colleagues are right in saying that more social programs would be lost if we eliminated universality, which gives rise to entitlement, I'd conclude that Canadian character has altered irrevocably. I'd like to think that Canadians would support a system that provides for our needy neighbours, the strangers sleeping in bus shelters and under bridges and families confined to motels and other substandard housing arrangements. It's as if we've placed these needy folks on the other side of the "Glass Wall."

I may be an optimist in this regard, but I continue to have faith in Canadian character. As for the stigma attached to receiving aid under exceptional circumstances, this would not be remedied by selective programming. Quite frankly, it was the guilt my parents and grandparents felt when they had to receive help that allowed the most needy in the community to receive the help they required. This guilt served as a control over the abuse of the system. Furthermore, it's hard to believe that guilt is a soul-crushing issue for those individuals who require assistance under exceptional circumstances. Certainly those citizens who receive aid after floods, ice storms, fires and tornadoes are relieved to receive a helping hand. They show little guilt. What they do show, however, is a need to reciprocate when another Canadian neighbour is in distress. As said earlier, a strong country is one that possesses a strong sense of reciprocal obligation.

In the early 1990s my wife undertook a project through St. Stephen's Settlement House in Toronto. The project was called Neighbours Helping Neighbours. The concept was simple. You did an inventory of people's skills and interests as well as special needs, and you matched them to those who had a need for specific assistance. Much to the surprise of my wife and St. Stephens, the premise for the program turned out to be wrong. Every time she matched a person with the skills and time required to help someone in need, the person in need wanted to reciprocate. Thus, an 80-year-old woman who needed some assistance around the house volunteered to read to preschool children at the local daycare centre. Other people who received help ended up serving meals at the local drop-in centre for homeless people. Government's professionally driven programs have been unable to capitalize upon this human instinct. The sense of reciprocal obligation cannot be purchased with public funds.

The most interesting example of reciprocal obligation occurred in a large residence for ex-psychiatric patients. A couple who lived in the residence ended up volunteering to help an isolated mentally ill person in their own building. He lived in the apartment just below theirs, and as he was so reclusive, they weren't aware of his existence. This example jarred my sense of how people receive help. It was after this that I turned to the concept of community capacity building as a means of strengthening the health and well-being of others.

It's situations like this that fuel my belief that the quality of both personal and collective obligation has not disappeared, even in an era when greed seems to have overcome our better judgment.

It's most unfortunate that this inherent quality of personal generosity among Canadians did not steel the resolve of senior government leaders to make required changes in the Canadian welfare state. The last major effort to effect fundamental change was that of Lloyd Axworthy, Canada's former minister of human resources (now there's a title open to thoughtful consideration). His initiative took place in 1993 and 1994. By that time, of course, it had become abundantly clear current approaches to Canadian social programming were in great difficulty.

I recall driving up from Montreal one afternoon to present a brief to the all-party parliamentary committee seeking consultation on this critical issue. As my young son had never seen the nation's capital, we went on a brief walkabout of the Parliament building. We stopped in front of the eternal flame, which bubbles up in celebration of the Canadian centennial — a sure child pleaser. A few minutes after discussing how gas can be ignited after bubbling through water, a 17-year-old homeless youth came over, took off his shoes, rolled up his pants and waded into the fountain. He startled me by scooping up coins. Needless to say, his behaviour prompted me to talk with the lad. He was one of those who had fallen through the webbing of our social-welfare net. Half an hour later I found myself making my presentation on behalf of the Canada Committee for the International Year of the Family to the parliamentary committee. I scrapped the polite opening of our brief and inserted this story about the youth in the fountain, a wonderful metaphor for all that's wrong with our system. It roused a few sleepy parliamentarians on the committee to look up from their notes. In fact, even the two committee members pouring themselves coffee and chatting at the back of the committee room stopped to listen to the introduction.

I went on to question why the largest national social-welfare expenditure had been removed from the reform exercise, namely, an overhaul of Canadian pension policy. I knew the answer to my own questions, of course. Axworthy realized that pension reform would be a major stumbling block, as it remains the most relevant social program for the baby-boom cohort. Rather than risk having his proposals shot down in flames, as there was too much public support for pensions, Axworthy removed the issue from the terms of reference for the overall project. It was easier for the committee to recommend an overhaul of university grants and programs affecting poor children and families than to tackle a program so popular with baby boomers. The committee members said nothing when I raised this concern. In the end, my remarks were duly noted, like most other presentations and briefs. Over the next few months the social-welfare reform project slowly faded into obscurity. Marc Lalonde had failed to alter the course of the social-welfare juggernaut. Now it was Lloyd Axworthy's turn to fail. And like Lalonde, Axworthy had little Cabinet support for what I consider a genuine personal effort.

What these failures of will, not intellect, created was an open field for the fiscal conservatives to run down the middle. Their underlying message was clear and readily understood. The country and provinces were in serious debt and operating deficits abounded. The only way to address this sad reality would be to slash social programming. Such an approach was much simpler than reforming the system itself.

Sixty years ago Canadians would have approached this issue in an incremental manner. "Who among us is in the greatest need and how can we tailor our resources to best address the needs of these specific groups?" It's on the basis of incremental reform that workers' compensation was introduced in 1914 and pensions for the elderly poor were introduced in 1929; it's also how unemployment insurance was first structured. At the same time it was within the character of Canadians to share in the care and nurturing of Canada's poor and physically and mentally challenged individuals. Citizens did this in countless formal and informal ways. It was a shared responsibility based upon a burning sense of reciprocal obligation. One of the last things Canadians of the era of the 1920s and 1930s considered was program universality. Programs didn't need to be universal to be accepted. It's only when greed became a strong element in the Canadian character that personal responsibility and collective responsibility became an unbalanced equation.

Rights replaced personal responsibility. This shift is most visible in the Canadian Charter of Rights and Freedoms, introduced by Pierre Elliot Trudeau. In the last 40 years we all began shouldering our way to the same trough, those with the greatest strength getting there first. A short distance away, of course, was another trough, one in which corporate subsidies were generously being sloshed out by governments. While the social-programs trough was the most visible, the corporate trough was being filled closer to the brim as many corporations had bigger appetites than the poor. By no means am I suggesting that all baby boomers or all corporations were at their selective troughs. Character runs deeper than this. As a result, some citizens and corporations, as illustrated earlier, continued their obligations and sought assistance only when their needs were dire.

When I think of this shift in character, I am reminded of a newsletter I received from the Fraser Institute. The lead article was on Milton Freedman's position on corporate charity. I had heard Milton Freedman speak on the subject at a small gathering in Colorado Springs, so was familiar with the rationale behind his position on corporate charitable giving. It went like this: "The role of the company is to make a profit. This profit is to be shared among shareholders. The shareholder determines whether or not to give some of these things to charity. Thus, it is wrong for companies to determine what charitable causes it wishes to support with shareholder earnings."

Two weeks after receiving this newsletter a corporate fundraising letter arrived in my mail from Michael Walker, president of the Fraser Institute. In this appeal he pointed out how the Fraser's research was benefiting corporations as well as ensuring that the voice of corporate Canada was being heard. He also mentioned, of course, that a generous charitable gift on the part of the corporation would result in a receipt, which could be used as a corporate tax benefit. I picked up the phone and called Michael Walker, with whom our foundation had done some work. "Michael," I said, "Isn't this request in direct contradiction to the lead article by Milton Freedman featured on the front page of your recent newsletter?" Michael's response was something to the effect that the views expressed by writers in the newsletter were not always the same as those official views of the institute. I don't mean to pick on Michael Walker, as he is an admirable guy whom I respect. The point of this short story is to point out the contradiction between rhetoric and practice. While many complained loudly and publicly about welfare handouts during the past 40 years, they were often the first folks to the trough when government aid was being handed out.

The more crucial point I wish to illustrate in the above example is that when national character changes, it does so in all sectors and in all social classes. The only exception to this observation is the character of minority groups recently arrived in Canada. Quite often these groups maintain their previous national character for many years. Thus, we often see a strong sense of interdependence among families and people within specific cultural groups. In the more advanced New Canadian cultures, we also witness strong collective interest in the welfare of the members of the culture. This collective interest in mutual welfare often results in the establishment of societies and fraternal organizations specific to the minority's culture or nationality. However, these exceptions do not outweigh the dominant influences of Canadian character.

To this point I have outlined when, how and why Canadian character changed over the years. It's not a bad thing or a good thing; it simply happened. Of course, it's much easier to look back and reflect on what happened than to look into the future. Nevertheless, readers will be dissatisfied if I don't suggest what might happen to our national character. It is easier to speculate on the evolution of Canadian social programs than on the evolution national character. There are some trends, however, and these give me cause for optimism.

The dominant baby boomers are now into their late 40s and 50s. In human development terms, this is a period that Erik Erikson described as one of reflection. One finally looks back on one's life and determines the achievements and failures and, more importantly, why these occurred. One's middle years are also a time for mentoring, a time to enjoy one's grandchildren, to speculate about their futures, and a time to consider the redistribution of one's wealth. I see this demographic change as being a major influence on the evolution of Canadian character. At a personal level the authoring of this book is an effort to make sense of what happened during my early and middle vocational years. I suspect that inevitably this pause to reflect will produce some positive changes. If the dominant age cohort begins to see the world differently, this can't help but influence other age cohorts. During the late 1960s and 1970s we witnessed youth culture reshaping national culture. Now the hippies and radicals have matured and are ready to have another crack at getting it right.

I also note with interest that the fastest growing service trend in Canadian society is self-help groups. Traditional social organizations and institutions have become petrified in their old ways. While many good organizations have attempted to renew their creativity through innovation, far too much of this innovation is simply a protective defence against becoming extinct.

At the same time, as I pointed out earlier, governments are nickel-and-diming social organizations to death through fastidious, nonsensical accountability. For too long they generously poured slop into the trough. Now they find themselves examining every nutritious morsel they are hand feeding to organizations and institutions. A consequence of this constipated thinking is that citizens are simply saying to themselves, we know what needs to be done, let's get out and do it. As a result, small acts of kindness and generosity are showing up among friends and neighbours, self-help groups and volunteers. For me, my eyes were opened by my wife's experience with her little project, Neighbours Helping Neighbours.

In my optimism I might go so far as to say that an eclipse temporarily darkened the underlying historic nature of Canadian character. Now our original character is re-emerging. It will be different, certainly, than the attitudes and values inculcated into me as a child of the Depression. Nevertheless, if you are in your early 40s or younger, you will likely experience a shift toward greater personal responsibility and obligation. In many ways your character may more accurately reflect the attitudes and values of your grandparents and great-grandparents than it does those of your parents, whose lives were dominated by chronic economic growth, materialistic expectation and power.

I have hope for the social future of Canadians. I still groan, however, at how our systems and organizations continue to plod a course toward extinction. They lack insight into how society really works. In addition they have no real capacity for being social entrepreneurs, and they fail to recognize the fact that people really do want to help their friends and neighbours. Governments are disconnected from the people they govern. Thus they do what they think is popular rather than what is required within the framework of the compassionate Canadian social contract.

Three years ago I did a study of child-welfare needs in northern British Columbia. It was obvious to local residents that the existing system was abysmal. The government of the day refused to participate in the study or to consider assistance in funding "For the Needs of Our Children." In the end I did it anyway, with modest support from a foundation for the proper publishing of the final report. I soon realized why government did not want the study undertaken. It turned out that the provincial government was not even living up to the basic tenets of the UN's Declaration on the Rights of Children. Our parents and grandparents recognized the need for a workable social contract involving both personal obligations as well as collective responsibilities. It's only then that you can address rights as part of the social contract. Under such circumstances, it's not a good time to be a creative and reflective person within what's left of the Canadian social-welfare state.

NOTES

1. Thomas Homer-Dixon, *The Ingenuity Gap* (Toronto: Vintage Canada, 2001) p 331.
2. Linda McQuaig, *The Wealthy Banker's Wife* (Toronto: Penguin Books of Canada, 1993).

Epilogue

It's taken me 65 years to move from my home in the Monarch Park neighbourhood of east Toronto to the side of Monarch Mountain in Canada's far northwest. The journey has spanned over half a century and close to 6,000 kilometres. Time and distance, however, are only two dimensions of my quest. The third dimension, and the most relevant to my life's journey, is the search for Canadian character. I have little choice about growing older. Driving with my friend Bruno Scorsone over 5,000 kilometres during the bitterly cold January of 1996 required a spirit of adventure, a little willpower and a modicum of stupidity. But experiencing my own character change, as well as witnessing the change in the general character of Canadians, has been a far more complex process than simply adding years to my life and kilometres to my car's speedometer. At one level Monarch Park and Monarch Mountain are simply locations on a map of Canada. However, they also represent a striking personal metaphor of my inner journey and the character journey of Canadians. The evolution of character is an infinite journey and a challenge to our future as a caring society in which reciprocal obligation is expressed in both our personal deeds and in our collective will.

It's now my fifth winter in the north. As I look out my office window the first rays of the sun are shining down on the snow-covered mountains and the spruce forest. The trees are glittering with hore frost from the ice fog that blanketed the mountainside overnight. Yesterday I was cross-country skiing on some splendid local trails. As I ambled along talking with a young friend about his hopes and dreams, the state of the economy and life in general, my two dogs stirred a small herd of woodland caribou in a spruce thicket. The caribou emerged just in front of us and trotted across the trail seeking protection in another spruce grove further up the mountainside. The two dogs looked dumfounded as they normally only raise a snowshoe hare. The dogs made a gesture at chasing the caribou, but not until the caribou were at a safe distance. Three leaps into the chest-deep snow were enough for them to regain their canine dignity. Meanwhile the long legs of the caribou had carried them out of view a couple of hundred metres away.

Our conversation turned to how these wonderful creatures look after one another against wolf packs that roam the area in the bitter sub-zero cold of midwinter. In many ways they are like the people of the Canadian north who come together to ward off dangers that threaten their existence. Historically, the Yukon has been a region of severe human hardship. During summer I've frequently hiked up the local creeks. Here and there is a deserted cabin, its windows long gone and its roof caved in. As I examine the rusting stove, the board bunks and the few simple household possessions scattered about, I am reminded of the depression of the early 1890s that inspired a flood of gold seekers to the Klondike and the Atlin region. They crossed the coastal mountains through the Chilcoot and White passes immediately west of Whitehorse. While a few people became prosperous, it was generally an era of broken dreams and dashed hopes. The plank headstones of the cemetery in Atlin speak eloquently to the hardship and deprivation of those early years. "Found dead on the trail." "Frozen to death." "Killed in a mining accident." "Shot dead, mistaken for a bear." These fading inscriptions are all that remain to mark the abbreviated lives of a number of former residents of the region. Some few kilometres away are the grave houses and plank headstones of the Taku River Tlingit First Nation. These headstones also reflect lives shortened by disease and hardship, particularly during the years following white settlement.

For the past few summers I've attempted to get into the head of one of those pioneers by playing the role of an Irish-Canadian miner who lived a reclusive life on the banks of Volcanic Creek. Having stumbled upon the miner's cabin, the ruins of which sit in a steep gorge located at the bottom of a narrow valley, I speculated about what life must have been like for someone who never experienced the direct rays of the sun, even in midsummer. Alas, Volcanic Joe, as I named my character, had become quite unhinged and kept an imaginary dog by the name of George as his sole companion. Having played the role performance after performance, part of me has become this reclusive soul from 1899. Thus, Volcanic Joe comes alive each summer Saturday night in a dinner mystery theatre performance aboard the M.V. *Tarahne*. The *Tarahne* was abandoned on the shore of Atlin Lake in 1931 and has been restored by the Atlin Historical Society.

I can now better appreciate what life must have been like for those Canadians who fled the depression of the 1890s and made their way to the northern goldfields. As in the Great Depression, there were no social services or welfare in 1898 or 1899 to ease the hardships. People depended upon one another for support when difficulties inevitably arose. It was the same on the Prairies, in the fishing villages of Atlantic Canada and in the poorer neighbourhoods of the towns and cities of Ontario and Quebec. While social support was generally inadequate and unreliable, particularly for the majority of people living at the margins, help that was forthcoming was genuinely compassionate. From these roots, of course, grew our vision for collective social programs, unemployment insurance and medicare being the most compelling. These and other social programs were implemented to redress consistency problems. In the new social order, however, it was expected that Canadians would continue to shoulder personal responsibility for their families, friends and neighbours. Alas, this component was gradually eclipsed with a dramatic change in Canadian character during most of my career.

I'm still actively seeking social justice and a better life for those who through no fault of their own have encountered severe hardship and/or personal difficulties. Today, despite continued high social-program costs, there are more homeless people on the streets, deeper levels of family poverty, more disabled people in need of basic support and far too many customers at the country's food banks. From late 1999 until 2001 I served as executive director of the Yukon Family Services Association, a vital agency that required major restructuring. Following that assignment I returned to my charitable foundation work and have been appointed to two federal committees. Most recently the Hon. Allan Rock, when he was minister of health, invited me to serve as the Yukon representative on his Advisory Council on Rural Health. I'm also keeping busy with Customs and Revenue Canada's Regulatory Table, which is helping to restructure the relationship between the federal government and the country's 72,000 charitable organizations.

My first love, however, remains closer to the frontline, where I served in the trenches for the past 45 years. As a member of the Whitehorse Committee on Homelessness, I am reminded how far we have yet to go in creating a compassionate and caring society.

I continue to be impressed with the countless number of professionals and volunteers who work with dedication and compassion to help alleviate suffering among Canadians in real need. They are doing a remarkable job, despite the systems in which they work. Hopefully their spirit will grow as Canadians begin to realize that far too many programs are being underutilized because of constipated thinking and planning. To change, however, governments must permit these workers and the organizations with which they work to take calculated creative risks. Innovation is urgently required before the entire service sector implodes upon itself. To achieve this critical change we need to ask ourselves two questions: "Does this make sense?" and "Are we addressing real human needs?" Currently the answer is negative to both questions. I firmly believe that Canadians continue to be a caring people both personally and collectively. This compassion must now be reflected in our behaviour and social programs. It will take courage and compassion, but these qualities are fundamental to our character. They may have been eclipsed for a while but they are not lost. Besides, we still have a capacity to ask the question, "Does this make sense?"

Index